WITNESS TO WAR

I watch a Special Forces unit get completely wiped out one day. From on top of an artillery bunker, we view the planned assault. Charlie has dug in on a low ridgeline between Khe Sanh and the Laotian border. Through high-powered binoculars mounted on a tripod, I watch the artillery prep fires. Barrage after barrage, our 105s and 155s churn up the dry dirt on the ridge. After a short silence, helicopters from the coast circle in and land right amongst the gook positions. As soon as the men start disembarking from the choppers, Charlie opens up. The sounds of gunfire reach me seconds after the fact.

It is just like watching a training exercise, except I can see puffs coming out the men's backs as they're hit. Dirt is being kicked up from the firing. The helicopters do not lift off; they sit with their rotor blades turning. I watch those brave doggies die trying to attack. After only a few minutes, the survivors climb back on the choppers and leave.

You do not win when you try to attack superior firepower that's dug in. Never.

WELCOME TO VIETNAM, MACHO MAN

Reflections of a Khe Sanh Vet

ERNEST SPENCER

BANTAM BOOKS
NEW YORK • TORONTO • LONDON • SYDNEY • AUCKLAND

The persons described herein represent composites of many individuals with whom the author was acquainted or had observed during the period covered. Any similarity to any person, either living or deceased, is not intended and is strictly coincidental.

This edition contains the complete text of the original hardcover edition.
NOT ONE WORD HAS BEEN OMITTED.

WELCOME TO VIETNAM, MACHO MAN

A Bantam Book / published by arrangement with the author

PRINTING HISTORY
Hardcover edition published by Corps Press.
Bantam edition / May 1989

Drawings by Greg Beecham.

Maps by Alan McKnight.

ISBN 0-553-27900-9

Published simultaneously in the United States and Canada

PRINTED IN THE UNITED STATES OF AMERICA

O   0 9 8 7 6 5 4 3 2 1

CONTENTS

NORTH VIETNAM

LAOS

Dong Ha
Demilitarized Zone
Con Thien
River
Quang Tri
Xe Pone
Khe Sanh
Hue
Phu Bai

THAILAND

Da Nang

Chu Lai

Quang Ngai

Dak To

Pleiku

Ia Drang River

CAMBODIA

Mekong River

CENTRAL

HIGHLANDS

Cam Ranh
Bay

Tan Son Nhut
SAIGON

DELTA

SOUTH CHINA SEA

SOUTH VIETNAM

Scale of Miles

0   50   100

PREFACE

I have written this account from the standpoint of the feelings I experienced during my tour in Vietnam. My life until Vietnam affected how and why I felt my war in my unique way. I believe, however, that my feelings were typical of those of line Marines in the late '60s and early '70s. Battles and operations are described as they affected feelings; this is not an account of my year in Vietnam.

Details are as I remember after the passage of 20 years. I have found, however, that a warrior's memory lasts a lifetime.

I have omitted negative writing about Marines who died. I would not consider myself a Marine if I spoke ill of our dead.

I have forgiven all whom I held in animosity, and I hope they have forgiven me. War is a time of exaggerated emotions. Love and hate were as close to us as life and death.

To the men of the 1st Battalion, 26th Marine Regiment

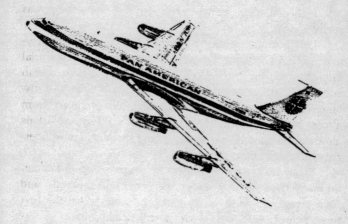

Boeing 707

Lock and Load: June 1967

I should have known going in that something was really wrong.

I'm looking out the window of a 707 at the countryside around Da Nang. I'm seeing what appear to be burial mounds. As we descend, I can see that they're bomb craters. Bomb craters all over the place. Off in the distance there is artillery fire. Grayish puffs of smoke form almost instantly. I don't know why, but artillery explosions always seem grayish—no matter where they hit. I'm wondering who might have stepped in it.

It has been such a long period of preparation for me. So many thoughts of war. So many mental rehearsals, and such intense feelings about going into battle for the first time. I am stoked, jacked up. A real macho man.

Coming down the aisle is a stewardess. You know, one of those types with the freeze-dried hairdo. She is telling the guys to buckle up. "I wouldn't want anyone getting hurt . . . ha, ha," she jokes.

Shit, I think, I'm all stoked, and this broad ruins it for me. This ain't right, I'm saying to myself. Something is wrong here. All the preparation for all these years, but I'm not prepared for *this*. None of the scenarios ever had women in it. This is supposed to be a man's thing; women aren't supposed to be in this. What the fuck is happening here?

WHO WAS I?

The Path

What led me to Vietnam? I never questioned the path, but I did think about it.

I think a lot, always have. I used to ask the heaviest why-type questions as a little kid. I used to go around the neighborhood where I grew up in Hawaii and rap with the housewives, who just loved my little ass. That was when I was only 4 years old.

My daddy told me that when I was 5 years old, the Marine Band came marching into the auditorium we were in, and I stood at attention. Oh Ernest, you fool! Something got to me too soon. The Marine Corps should be kept away from young boys.

I'm not saying the Marines wouldn't get guys, though; I know I was the type who would have gone anyway. Being the Corps was my reality, my destiny. I was the type who was so certain about the Corps that I needed to have my bell rung early so that I could get on with my life.

For some reason I fought a lot as a kid. I'm honestly not

sure why. They say I had a cockiness about me—I guess it came from my certainty. I was one of those kids who thought that the sun shone out his ass.

Some people would say that I was a borderline juvenile delinquent. I don't know what it was about me that trouble liked. If I was one of 30 people on a bus when trouble got on, guess who trouble would sit next to? Things just happen a certain way when you're young and don't know any better.

That's young-kid macho. When you play macho that way, guys are going to take you on and it usually ends in a fight. I never picked fights, but I sure got into them. That was cool macho, and I was cool. Always cool. Don't know why, maybe it's in my genes. I can't remember anyone teaching me that.

Maybe man just has a violent nature. Maybe we're not realistic with ourselves. We're always trying to find meaning and justification and acceptance for our actions. Maybe some things defy reason and just are. Like man and violence. Maybe all we know is violence.

My Church

Being born a Catholic and being raised a Catholic are two different things. I was both. The imprint was imperfect, but by the time I was 5 years old my conscience had been rewired Catholic style.

The Catholic Church depended on conscience. Take the collection, for example: Just give what your conscience said to. Of course they tried their best to get into your conscience. Catholics are cold, I tell you. They did collections with baskets that were attached to long poles. The dudes would march—not walk, but march—to the front of the church, do the dip (the genuflection), and start working the crowd. If it was a packed house during a Sunday prime-time mass, they'd also have guys working the crowd from the back of the church forward.

Conscience meant guilt. Your ass was liable for all kinds of punishment. All the good stuff was a mortal sin, and a mortal sin could put your ass in hell. The priests reminded you all the time when the collection plate went around that it was them saving your ass, too.

Priests were tight with The Man. They turned The Man into the wafer in a magic show every day at mass. You could eat God every day, if you did the routine. I never believed it. But I was like Pascal, the philosopher. I gambled that it might be true. If those strange black-robed magicians were right about what happened after death, I wanted to cover my bets.

I guess I've always had a weird relationship with death. I think that it all started when I was an altar boy. Death was a big deal in the Catholic Church, which had a ritual for every stage of dying. If there was enough time, you could get an oil-job first. They called it the last rites.

The first service after death was the rosary, which was followed by mourning. As an altar boy, I learned different types of mourning because different races mourn differently. White people wore black. Yellow people wore white. The other races wore anything they had. It seemed as if only the whites and yellows had any money.

How could I tell who had the money? The coffin. People were keeping up with the Joneses right into the grave. As if the worms really cared. I remember doing one man who was laid out in a $5,000 coffin. That was a lot of money in the 1950s. The family gave each altar boy $5

5

after the funeral. "Of course you can keep the money," the priest told me. "Or, you could donate it to the Church." His eyes bore in on me as he said it. Five bucks was more money than I had ever earned. I had seen what had happened to that stiff, though, and I just didn't want to risk it. The priest took my $5 and didn't even say thank you on behalf of God.

You get smug doing funerals as a kid because all you do is old people. It makes you think that you'll be around for a long time. The body would be laid out in the casket with the lid up. Although that first view of the stiff always puckered my ass right up, in time I got so professional that I could tell the good undertakers from the bad ones. The good undertakers could do some old bird and make her look like she'd just had her hair done and was taking a nap. The bad ones made the stiff look like she'd just been through a car wash. Bad? I remember one little kid peering into the coffin and saying, "That ain't my grandpa!"

One altar boy carried incense in an urn; the other carried a bucket of holy water and a hand sprinkler. (You usually worked in pairs as altar boys.) After the priest swung an urnful of burning incense around the stiff, he'd sprinkle the body with holy water. I always winced, thinking the guy would twitch or sit up and say, "Hey! Knock it off!"

I would have said, "See, I told you we should've driven a stake in his chest!"

Can you believe that I used to be an altar boy? I wasn't into bullshit even then, though; I never learned my lines for mass. Swear to God. I never learned my lines—I just hummed "Latin." Only one priest ever called me on it. This priest stopped and said, "What?" I looked up at him and rolled my eyes back like I was sick and going to faint. He told me to leave the altar and go to the sacristy. I didn't put any nickels in the candle slot on my way, either. I was saving my money to spend on girls.

Women have always had an enormous amount of influence on me. Nuns could get me to do the dip just by pressing a clicker. They called them crickets. A cricket was a little metal tab that clicked when the nun bent it with her thumb. It clicked again as it bent back to the original position.

Click-click . . . down onto the right knee, always the right knee. Forget the British—my nuns were Irish nuns. If it was a formal dip, you had to cross yourself—with the right hand, always. First to the forehead, then to the chest, the left shoulder, and the right. You had to do all that exactly because God was watching. He was up there in the front of the church hiding in this domed thing on top of the altar. Spooky place.

Clickers were used by the nuns because God did not like women talking in His church. Only men could talk in church.

Kids got restless in church, especially boys. God help you if a nun saw you fooling around. She'd walk up to you and establish eye contact. A nun could burn holes in you just by looking at you. Talk about giving someone the whammy!

Nuns were heavy. They could get you to do things without saying a word. I learned that from nuns: the power of silence. That, and the stare—I learned that from them too. Some of them could hypnotize. Nuns weren't bullshitting, either; they believed. You've got to believe to make your eyes work that way.

Formal education in a Catholic school starts with nuns pulling and twisting ears. You graduate to high school and out-and-out beatings. I went to an all-boys Catholic high school. Carmelite priests and brothers were our teachers and advisors. Those guys were into self-flagellation when I knew them, and you just know that any man who kicks his own ass is going to have no problem doing yours. Priests, brothers, and lay teachers vented their inner frustrations on the students in rituals of torture. Discipline, they called it.

The formal version of discipline consisted of swats. Most priests would use their thick belts on us—belts like razor strops. But one used a sawed-off golf club, and another had a paddle in the shape of a hand. Swats were usually given for verbal infractions—mouthing off. The number of swats you received was directly proportional to the volume of laughter your vignette generated.

Discipline became a macho thing. If you were the guilty party, you were required to hold your ankles while being whipped in front of the class, and if you let go of your ankles, you were considered a sissy. If you were real macho, you didn't even flinch. You could get up to 20 swats for major infractions. Guys cheered you if you took them all without flinching. Sometimes you even got a standing ovation afterward.

What do high-school guys with no girls around do wrong? Everything. We'd egg those priests and brothers on. Push them. Find their weaknesses. Test them. We were flat-assed, all-the-time wired, and horny. I perfected my crudeness in Catholic boys' high school.

I remember the time I borrowed one of those new wristwatches with an alarm and set it off in class. Brother came flying down the aisle, and the guy next to me started laughing. Brother punched the guy right on his ear. I didn't make a sound; the guy didn't say a thing either. We accepted justice that way. The guy was macho. He didn't squeal. There was nothing he could do about the hit he took, so why mess his buddy up?

I learned about booze from those priests and brothers. They must have been terribly lonely men. A lifetime is a long wait for a reward of eternal happiness, especially when they believed that anyone could qualify by just asking for forgiveness. Yep, you could mess up all your life, ask forgiveness at the end, and still go to heaven. It must have been living with that belief that turned them into drunks. You could smell them in the morning and again after lunch. Zombies, some of them. In the afternoons some would be red-eyed drunk.

Boys use any justification they can to turn on or mess up. If the priests drank, it had to be OK, right? Don't get me wrong, they were good teachers. They were educators. But when it came to drinking, they gave me a hint of reality versus reason. They talked good, but they were boozers. Was it the faith that made them talk good, or was it the booze that let them hang on and keep talking? I got the feeling all the time with those guys that somehow, somehow, they knew their life was wrong. I saw that in them—it was in their eyes. They knew life was not the way they wanted it to be.

Priests often went into the seminary right after grammar school. Imagine going in and locking yourself away like that when you're only 15 years old. You wake at 30 or 40 and realize you've been had. First, last, and foremost you're just a man, but being a priest is all you've ever known and done. To be trapped that way—I can relate to that.

Playing Macho

I wanted to be a man who was macho. Not for what macho would give but for what macho itself was. A feeling. A belief. The certainty of living without question. In the Marine Corps the macho goal was so simple and clean: I wanted to be perceived as the best by those I was responsible for. My men. My kingdom. I wanted to be a feudal prince. A god. A warrior god living in a kingdom of death.

The worst thing you could call a fellow Marine was a cunt; we were supposed to be men. Being a Marine was all about being a macho man. Macho is not just played by military types, though. Anybody can play macho.

Macho can also mean bullshitting yourself and others as much as possible. The problem with playing macho is that macho is about being afraid—afraid of rejection. It is a desire to be loved, wanted, and respected. Being macho is depending on others for your status. A macho guy is the counterpart of the woman who is locked into how she is perceived by others rather than who she herself is. There's not much difference between a macho guy and a woman who keeps trying to find happiness with a senseless jerk rather than in herself. Macho is being afraid to look at yourself and laugh—to laugh for caring so much about what others think. Fear of rejection gets a woman rejection after rejection; it gets a guy killed.

The Futility of Reason

Philosophy was my college major. The problem with being a trained philosopher is that you don't just accept things as easily as other people do. Most people are inside

10

out: If they're in control of themselves, it's their act that counts and what they perceive to be their act goes. A philosopher, on the other hand, tries to get close to understanding by going outside himself.

I tried the classic philosopher's route to understanding. I honed my objectivity. I flexed my powers of analysis. But it all became semantics after a while. Philosophy was words worked over and tossed in the vacuum of the college environment.

The college environment was surreal. You read Aristotle and Thomas Aquinas—all the thinkers of ancient times. As far as I could tell, it was the same times. I couldn't see where mankind had learned a thing. Everything was the same except the clothes.

By my second year in college, I was overwhelmed by the futility of reason as an effective force in life. From the historical perspective I could see that reason didn't mean didley shit—reason was philosophy read by a couple of frumpy-looking professors. Strife was what was really out there. The lack of order in the world stood out so clearly to me. My history was the history of strife. I was born during World War II, and my earliest recollections were of the Korean War. How could reason expect to win when it didn't get any air time? All my heroes were warriors—actual warriors or the silver-screen variety.

Disillusioned by reason, life did not make sense to me. I was lost. I was drawn to the Marine Corps by the sense of belonging. The Corps also offered me the chance to confront life rather than read about it. I could confront life by going to the edge, or at least what I perceived as the edge: Existence itself.

Why this penchant for violence as a means? Is it a means? Maybe violence is an end in itself. If it weren't, why has man let it go on so long? Man perpetuates violence with the excuse that it's someone else's fault. Only the crazy ones take responsibility for violence.

Well, I must have been crazy, then, because I did it voluntarily. I joined the Marines.

GETTING THE BULLSHIT OUT

Life is assimilating what is thrown at you according to the circumstances at the time. I was so easy that I bit the first time the hook was thrown at me. If Marine recruiters had hit me up in high school, who knows what would have happened? I think I would have joined up, missed the war years, and become an attorney. I suffer so the world doesn't; I do a war and society gets one less attorney.

I didn't get hustled in high school because they didn't need Marines then. Uncle Sam sent the crimps (the recruiters) out when I was in college. I joined the Marine Corps Reserve in 1963.

The war was really just beginning for America when I was in Officers' Basic School. During the summer of '65, we'd sing about going to Nam. As we ran in formation, guys made up rhymes about it. With my classmates I watched the Marines land at Da Nang on TV. We hoisted glass after glass in toast to the Marines that night—a barful of fellow 2nd lieutenants, cheering. What energy! Macho is so easy to play when you're just standing in a bar drinking beer.

But as winter came and our graduation neared, many of my classmates began to change. They expressed strong reservations about going off to war. At that time, in 1965, much of the fancy reasoning about the propriety of the war had not yet surfaced. These guys were just flat opposed to the possibility of getting their asses waxed. It dumbfounded me. "What the fuck did you join the Marine Corps for, asshole," I'd ask them, "the uniform and the chance to impress pussy?"

Most, like me, had joined in the early 1960s. Like me they were commissioned upon graduation from college. It shocked me to see the change in attitude of so many officers who had done boot camp with me. They had been so sure and macho then.

"I got a wife to think about now," one said to me.

I gave him the standard Marine response: "If the Marine Corps wanted you to have a wife, they would have issued you a wife. Since they didn't, she's your problem."

As time passed, I became a member of a distinct minority, one of the voluntary grunts (a voluntary infantryman). Why in the fuck would anyone become a Marine if it weren't to be an infantry officer, I thought. My small group would have gone and fought anything. Not just anyone, anything. We were so stupid, we would have taken on a herd of elephants if that was the mission assigned.

When graduation neared and orders were assigned, my group reaped a perverse vengeance. One month before graduation MOSs (Military Occupational Specialties) were assigned along with duty stations. Most of my class at Officers' Basic School became supply officers, and all the guys who chose supply got 3 months of additional school and orders for Vietnam. I never thought I'd see Marine officers cry, but some did. They wanted so to be thought of as heroes, but they were unwilling to pay the price. Cruel bastards that we were, we tacked notes to their doors: WELCOME TO VIETNAM, TOUGH GUY! Because they went right to Vietnam, some of those guys ended up doing two tours in Nam on their 3-year hitches. Payback is a motherfucker, isn't it? I graduated from Officers' Basic School in December 1965. My orders were for Camp Lejeune, North Carolina.

They promoted us fast. By 1966 the names of my classmates who became infantry officers were already appearing as KIA (Killed in Action). Before I even went to Vietnam, half the infantry officers in my class had been killed.

I reported to the 2nd Battalion, 2nd Marine Division, "Swamp" Lejeune in January 1966, where I was assigned as platoon commander, 2nd Platoon, Golf Company.

We trained out in the field, teaching Marines how to kill in the bush. I always taught mine to do it close. I taught them to set up a tight ambush and to always leave yourself a bug-out route because in an ambush you never know if you're biting off too much. I also taught them to stay close to resupply points. Never cut yourself off from resupply.

I must have taught killing in a past life—it came to me so naturally. I must have been an Indian because I like it so close. I want to see the guy I do. I want him to see me. If you're going to do someone, you owe him that much. Don't get me wrong. When the time came, I took 'em any way I could. But I'd look. If I had a choice.

I hated garrison duty. I always hated defense. Yes, I always believed the Marine saying: Attack first, hit first. When in doubt, attack. But wouldn't you know it? All I got was defense shoved down my throat. I was a 2nd lieutenant and was assigned as defense counsel.

I spent a lot of time at the brig, listening to liars blowing smoke up my ass. "No sir, Lieutenant, I promise. If they release me, I won't run away again."

Some didn't lie. Some looked me straight in the eye and said, "Sir, I don't want any part of this fucking outfit any longer." Well, I'd speak for those young fools and plead whatever for them. Then I'd watch my fellow officers find them guilty. I lost every case I did. All my deserters got 6, 6, and a kick—6 months in the brig at hard labor, 6 months loss of pay, loss of rank, and a bad-conduct discharge. Some of those stupid shits thanked me for getting them that sentence. They thought they finally saw a light at the end of the tunnel. In fact, the higher court of appeals always sent all those guys straight to Nam.

Defense. I was a defense counsel setting guys up for war. How fitting that I got to be with those I sent to Nam, where most of what we did was defense.

Within a few months my battalion was sent to Cuba. Guantanamo Bay. Spring 1966. Went by ship and got to see the squids—the Navy—up close. Fuck the Navy.

I remember the Marine I shipped out with, the platoon commander of 1st Platoon. Tarzan-type guy. Possible lifer. Bachelor. Not fully developed mentally or emotionally. Tarzan was crazy. I would not have been surprised if he had gone on a one-man night raid into Cuban-held territory.

Officers dine formally on Navy ships. Senior officers at one end of a long table, junior officers at the other end. Tarzan and I were with the Navy ensigns. An ensign is the most junior Navy officer. Those ensigns still had pimples.

106mm Recoilless Rifle

They were all dorks. Skinny dorks or fat dorks, all the squids were dorks.

Tarzan and I used to act crazy in front of the squids. The ensigns down at our end of the table didn't know what to make of us. I was doing one of those dogs-that-just-starts-to-snarl numbers: top lip on one side lifted in a half smile, facial muscles twitching.

The Navy had Filipino stewards who served the meals. Saltiest suckers in the world, those stewards could teach a Paris waiter how to fuck with people. When the stewards reached Tarzan, the dish of potatoes had only a Navy portion left—a couple of potatoes each. Tarzan asked for seconds. The steward said, "There's no more!" Tarzan's eyes went off like lights at a drag strip. The next night when the steward came by with a plate full of pork chops,

Tarzan took all but two. The steward got pissed, but he took one look at Tarzan and one look at me and backed off. We got all the seconds we wanted after that. The stewards even used to ask us if we wanted more.

At breakfast Tarzan and I ate toast, potatoes, four eggs, and eight pieces of bacon and drank three glasses of milk. If war didn't do us, coronary would. I think some of the ensigns started skipping meals because we upset them so much. But Tarzan and I never missed a meal. Sea duty was eating, sleeping, and gambling at night. That's all we did. We worked hard when we were ashore, but at sea—fuck it. Goddamn Navy gets paid for that.

Young buck at that age could do all sorts of shit to himself and still feel great. I weighed 162 pounds. Ate every chance I got. I smoked a pack and a half a day. Drank mostly beer—twelve or more at party time. Felt great, strong. Was cocked and ready to go off, and the attitude served me well.

You have to fight for your turf in the Marines. You've got to fight for your respect. Nobody gives a 2nd lieutenant any respect. That's why he's got to act so tough—everybody treats him like a joke.

Those ensigns knew their places. They were invisible, just the way they were supposed to be. They did bullshit jobs. But a 2nd lieutenant in the infantry is different. He is the link to the men, the men who fight. He is a joke to all above him. Whether he is a joke to those under him is his call. He decides. He decides by showing his men that he is together. You don't bullshit Marines. Not for very long, you don't. Not about some things.

I remember a guy I'd done boot with in the early '60s. He was a big, mean football player. Straight to Nam he went. When I saw him again, I was touring the firing ranges at Camp Lejeune as a safety officer. Football Joe was working a unit firing 106mm recoilless rifles. He was in a 40-foot tower. I climbed up via a long, outside wooden ladder. He recognized me first—I guess I had not changed to him, but boy had he changed for me.

What a skeleton he was. His once-muscled beefy frame was gaunt. His face was so much thinner. He was real nice and talked softly. Nam had definitely changed him. He showed me his hit. Looked like a zipper. The scar went from his gut to his neck. No more football for him. You don't need games after that. I thought at the time that he was different than I. Dream on, Ernest.

In Cuba I did not put up with any shit in my platoon. From anyone. I'd hit a guy if he sassed me. We were not supposed to. Hitting was a no-no for officers.

I did not have experienced NCOs (noncommissioned officers) in Cuba; the NCOs were all in Vietnam, where they were needed. As a result, I had to be both sergeant and lieutenant. I'd get right in a guy's face when I ate his ass. He'd stand there at attention, and I'd go at him. Sloppiness was what pissed me off the most. Sloppy tactics. Sloppy attitude. I was up. I wanted my men ready to kill. Kill? In Cuba? Cuba was a political joke. I was all gung-ho.

2nd lieutenants should have time to break in that way. Leading men takes a feel. They should have time to work with men under noncombat conditions. If I had been dropped off in Khe Sanh as a 2nd lieutenant right out of Basic School, I'd have been a KIA for sure. From the field standpoint my training was perfect.

Doing Vietnam the way I did gave me the edge. Not just in rank, but in maturity. I got the bullshit out of myself in Cuba. I was more ready for Vietnam than some soldiers. I was lucky. Some luck.

SLIDING RIGHT INTO IT

Green-Ass Marine

Different places have different smells. Have you ever noticed how you can smell the flowers when you first arrive in Hawaii? That's the first thing I notice when I've been away from the Islands awhile. It's the flowers that I always notice first. Fragrant smells of flowers on warm breezes. The fragrance feels soft, smells soft. It almost tastes soft.

Da Nang smells like old piss and burlap coming off a heater fan. This place is hot. Hot and different. I feel it stepping off the plane. Hot, sticky wetness. You can't run far or fast in this shit.

The bivouac area next to the airstrip is the staging area for Marines going upcountry. It looks just the way I thought it would—dirty, dusty tents and aimless green-ass Marines walking around with a dumb-fuck look on their faces. As though they're not sure all this is for real. I am sure. Sure as a motherfucker.

I had made myself a promise before I left for Vietnam. While in Vietnam I would never question my reasons for being there. I knew only the world and had never experienced combat. Fear, I thought, might cloud my reasoning. In the end, the crucible of war would show me what was right. War is such truth. Peace is such fallacy. I am so sure of myself. This is it. The whole thing. One tour.

This is my shit starting, mine alone. I can feel myself sliding right into it. Just easing right into it.

Nearby is a slop chute (a bar) for staff NCOs and officers. I am tight with alcohol. If I don't have anything else to do, I do what a lot of Marines do: I try to see how fast I can destroy my kneecaps. That's how I can always tell I'm drunk: My knees disintegrate. I try to get up from a bar stool, and my hands have to save my ass because my knees and lower legs faint on me. Booze and macho seem to go together. Or is it macho and booze?

The bar is nothing more than a tin-roofed shack. It is raised off the ground on stilts and about the size of a small classroom. Cold beer is the only alcoholic beverage—Miller in cans. Someone must have bought somebody because Miller High Life is the only beer the Marines serve.

I am a grunt. An infantryman. We are dirty, ugly, and stupid looking, like Marines are supposed to look. None of those bullshit poster shots. Real Marines look like side-show attractions or circus clowns without makeup.

Most grunts have a sense of humor. Granted, it is usually perverse, but each guy has his own gig. If you are a grunt and not a funny grunt, you don't make it; everyone gets on you. Being funny is survival. Grunts don't argue out in the field. They rib the hell out of each other or they kill each other, but they don't fight. Being funny is the safety valve. It makes perfect sense. Arguing's for back in the world. Killing's for real.

It does not take very long for me to get drunk in the heat. A Vietnamese bar girl keeps trying to get me to fuck her. I'm so waxed by now that every time I try to see what she looks like, I've get a double-vision shot going. An NCO keeps trying to slip me a condom. I'm going to worry about a dose of clap when I got one fucking year of war ahead of me? I leave the bar by myself.

Our tents are by the runway, three fourths of the way down. Inside my tent are sandbag walls 3 feet high and dusty cots on a dirt floor. No bedding. I fold my trousers and shirt for a pillow. I lie there in my skivvies, listening to the fighters take off.

When they come by, the planes are just starting to lift off. They're really screaming, engines blasting afterburners. It's so loud it shakes me inside. It is macho music to me. It is heat for Charlie (the Vietcong). Give them heat, I'm thinking . . . go motherfuckers. Even though the paired takeoffs are continuous and at less than 2-minute intervals, I have no trouble sleeping. Good sleep, macho sleep. Take-it-as-it-comes sleep.

My checkout at 3rd division headquarters is a vague blur. A major tells me I will be going to Khe Sanh. The way he says it, the name sounds like *caisson*—an ammunition wagon and hearse. The location of the place catches my attention. Khe Sanh is in the northwestern corner of South Vietnam, right next to Laos and North Vietnam. On the map I'm looking at, it looks like Laos is a four-wood golf shot away, and North Vietnam is within artillery range. Major battles are just ending on Hills 881 and 861 at Khe Sanh. The hills are now occupied by Marines. I am think-

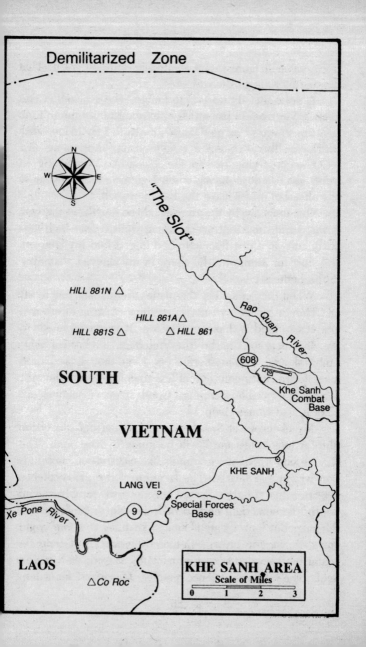

ing to myself, Ernest, you wanted in and you got it. That fucking place is all the way in.

It's the first time I feel the edge. The realization that I am going right in causes it. I am going to a line unit (an infantry unit) that is at Khe Sanh, the 1st Battalion, 26th Marine Regiment.

I go by helicopter to Khe Sanh. What a knock-out view. I'm a candy-ass nature lover. I remember Hawaii in the '50s, before it got messed up, and Khe Sanh reminds me of it. Khe Sanh is gorgeous. Mountains; lush green; white waterfalls everywhere; deep, deep valleys. Rivers with almost blue water. A place like that can swallow you.

While watching this from the helicopter, I start visualizing closeup shoot-outs. Macho is a psych job. You've got to psych, or focus, yourself. I visualize close-in firing because this is jungle. In a jungle, people shoot close— real close . . . touch close. I want to be ready. I've got to expect it to go off real close. Long-range rifle fire is jacking off. Real close is pussy.

When I arrive my battalion is south of Khe Sanh on Route 9. They had been ambushed by units of the NVA (North Vietnamese Army) earlier, in the morning. I have to wait for the battalion commander and operations officer to return from the ambush site.

Infantry officers in the lower ranks (under major) are in very short supply now. A dozen or so of my class of over 200 became infantry officers. Most became supply officers or went to flight school. Even in the Marines, the fightingest branch of the armed forces, less than 10 percent of the guys are in line units. Most of the others just help the grunt get there so he can get his ass kicked, or feed him and supply him so he can get his ass kicked for a long time, or process him out after he's had his ass kicked enough.

I am an infantry officer 0302, a 1st lieutenant. I have no doubts about my leadership ability. People seem to follow me easily. I'm hot shit; Billy Joe Bad-Ass himself. I'm natural and for real. Men can see that in each other.

I spend my first night at Khe Sanh in what amounts to the officers' tent at the headquarters area. I notice something real strange. I know some of the guys I spend the night with—I'd served with them back in the world. These guys are just finishing their tours in Nam and are getting ready to go home. I realize that Marines are different than your standard McDonald's-eating jerk-off, but these guys are moving and acting strangely even for Marines. It's their eyes and the way they laugh. Not really laughing, it's more an uncontrolled, almost apologetic giggle. Their eyes never look straight at anything and are always moving. I feel out of synch with these guys. It is like being at a party where everyone is stoned but you.

The first night is cold and foggy. When I am alone, it all feels as if it is coming together perfectly. I can't imagine a better way to break in. Cold, fog, foreboding, coming, coming on. It seems as though time itself is changing. Days, weeks, hours—they become irrelevant. The situation, the surroundings—they are becoming my focus, like time spent with a mistress. I feel her presence. I do not know her yet, but I feel myself moving—flowing—toward her. I am not afraid.

I must cease being the person I had been back in the world. No one I knew back in the world has any part in this. I cannot think of them because they are a part of the world. This is not the world. I know that. Standing there in the mist and fog at Khe Sanh, I know.

My mistress, war, has laid such a beautiful trap in her seduction of me. She seduces me in the beauty of the mountains, and I am so vulnerable to her.

Each man has his own relationship with war. I wonder what the guys who don't want to be there feel like. That would be heavy emotions. Like panic. Panic out in the open. All the time. You would go loony real quick if that's how you felt.

But for me, what a relief war is. All the chicken shit is over. Now I'd get to be the Marine I'd always dreamed of being—the best man I can be. As far as the Marines are concerned, that means being a killer. No more back-in-the-world bullshit.

I meet with the colonel and the operations officer the next morning. The colonel's using an old French bunker as his quarters. Quite plush. Cement walls and floors, real stairs. Narrow slits for windows at ground level and a nice thick roof. I look around and think that I wouldn't want to be in this palace if shit hit. It is too big. A bunker should be tight, like pussy, if it's going to be good. You want the walls real close. You want to just fit and barely be able to breathe. A bunker is like a target where any hit on the target is a bull's-eye. So you don't give the cocksucker a big target unless you like fucking with death.

The operations officer says they like my OQR (my Officer Qualification Record). Almost all my service had been line time in command positions. Fleet Marine time. He asks me what I want. I tell him I just want in the field with a rifle company. "How about commanding Delta Company?" he asks. I almost come in my pants. You have got to understand what it means to a 24-year-old guy who's macho to be made a commanding officer of a rifle company in combat. He is Jesus Christ himself. The best I thought I'd do was to make executive officer. Being an executive officer is like being vice-president—you only do something when the CO (the commanding officer) dies. But here I am, a 1st lieutenant in command of a rifle company. I flash on stepping up too high, but tell myself not to question. Be. Just be what comes. Do not question, just do what you've prepared yourself to do.

Delta 6

There are four rifle companies in my infantry battalion: Alpha, Bravo, Charlie, and Delta. I will command Delta; therefore, my battalion call sign is Delta 6. Delta Company is holding Hill 861, which is west of Khe Sanh. I'm going right out on my own, just the way I like it. I've always doubted the opinions of others when it comes to doing things. I am more certain, more sure. I trust myself more than I trust others. I guess that's why I have great difficulty following instructions.

I am met at the landing zone on Hill 861 by the departing commander of Delta Company. He is a civilized, macho, salty-ass Marine. John Wayne couldn't have played it better. This guy is a mustang (an ex enlisted man). He is a tough son of a bitch, but the year in Nam has done him in. You can see the fatigue in his eyes.

I quickly decide that I will not change what is obviously working. I stay with the salty-ass captain for two days. He pulls a surprise inspection of the hill for my edification. One of those old-fashioned Marine Corps throw-shit-around, I'm-all-pissed inspections. He really lays into the lieutenants about their attitudes.

I deeply appreciate the favor he shows me. He allows

me, the new skipper who now commands seasoned platoon commanders, a chance to lead quietly and slowly. We discuss the strengths and weaknesses of the platoon commanders. According to him, two are excellent and one is poor. We are like two trainers discussing the fighting capabilities of their boxers. "He has a good head on him." "He leads well." "He's sharp, very sharp." Well, we are fighters, aren't we? I listen. I listen my ass off. I want to know as much as possible about who I am getting to do the fighting for me. Officers are supposed to lead and not actually do any of the fighting themselves. That was the tradition before Vietnam, anyway. Vietnam had already changed a lot of traditions.

I decide that I will defer to my lieutenants' recommendations whenever possible. I assign the missions and objectives, but I leave the maneuver decisions to them. The two good ones, anyway.

I feel bad about the one that is not right. He is such a nice guy. A warm, sincere, genuine person. But this is not the place for nice-guy platoon commanders. The two other platoon commanders and the executive officer let me know right off: They don't think he's worth shit. I decide to wait awhile. I want to give the man the benefit of my own judgment of him. I just get here and right off I've got to play God.

That's what a company commander is. God. Any man who can decide who goes out every day to die has got to be God.

FOG AND CLOUDS

Hill 861

From atop Hill 861 you can see Khe Sanh below. To your right is Laos. To your left is the slot, the long valley that runs all the way into North Vietnam. At your back are Hills 881 North and 881 South. Hill 861 is the first in the series of hills to the northwest of Khe Sanh. All the area is supposed to be devoid of friendlies. No civilians. Everything is fair game.

Khe Sanh sits on a high plateau. Deep, deep valleys surround the northern side. To the south of Khe Sanh, it is relatively flat to where a river forms the border between South Vietnam and Laos, then high mountains dominate. Co Roc sits like the Rock of Gibraltar just inside Laos. Hills 861 and 881 South are both manned by a company of Marines and used as fire bases.

Our patrols stay close. The memory of the recent battles fought here dictates a caution, a leeriness. We are ordered to go no more than a few thousand meters out. Hill 881 North is visible from both 861 and 881 South. 881

North is Mr. Charles's fire base. The thing even looks ominous. I go up it more than once. It puckers my ass every time. It has as much history to me as anything. It is feeling.

The first weeks on 861 are exciting. The sights, the newness of it all. Being out there and all alone like that. My own fire base, just me. If you don't get hit right away, you can really get into the lifestyle. The clouds. The fog. The rain. The mist. The streams, rivers, and waterfalls. Khe Sanh is about water. You can look out at it or be completely enveloped. Water as life. My life as death. It is a very heavy place. My childhood leaves me at Khe Sanh.

Monsoon

The early months are long periods of fog and dampness. Our trench lines keep flooding at the base of the hill. We have to put in culverts to drain them.

Sheets of water falling in a constant patter all about. Men in ponchos slogging around with their heads bent forward like penitent monks. Clicking sounds of raindrops hitting my helmet. The smells of dampness and mildew. My boots mildew overnight with a fine whitish-green dust like powder on the toe. Sandbags give off a pungent aroma of burlap and oil. Musty odors. I can almost see the dampness.

My hands and feet start looking like the Grand Canyon after a while. They turn gray and wrinkled. I cannot believe they are my hands and feet. I swear they belong to some other motherfucker—someone who has a very bad defect.

It is so cold and wet some mornings when I inspect

the hill. My dick and balls say to me, "Hey, fuck it, asshole, we're going up inside your crotch until you get outta this shit." I stop and share a smoke with a guy just finishing his watch at a machine-gun position. We have to tuck our chins up close to our chests and under our helmets to protect the cigarette from the driving rain. The guy and I stand there with our shoulders hunched up around our ears, leaning into the wind and rain. Rain dripping down my face and back, we talk for a few moments. I ask him if he has a girlfriend, and if he does, what her name is. Or where he is going on R&R. Or how much time he has left to do in Nam, Just pleasantries.

Waterfalls. Falling waters. Rain, rain, incessant falling rain. I am drenched beyond what I'd ever imagined wet could be. But when I can put the rain out of my mind and get beyond my personal sense of wetness, I begin to know the beauty of the rain in the sounds it makes. The rain on open ground sounds like the crackling of a fire. Rain falling through trees sounds like thousands of rushing waves. The rain becomes a symphony played just for me. Enchanting sounds. The droplets blending into the forest with the sounds of the rain.

Smells

Before Nam I never gave odors much thought. Sure, you always remember particular aromas because they signal a special time. The smell of Thanksgiving dinner is a memory that stands out. And the scent of Christmas trees. But the rest of the smells just seem to blend away with your past.

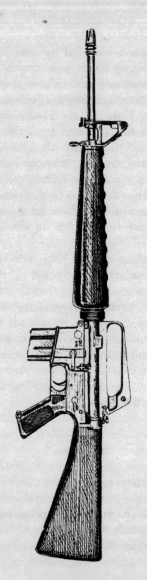

M-16

Nam is Nam because of its smells. Nam gets right inside your nose and stays there.

I am bewildered and delighted at first. Smells keep unlocking childhood memories, which come tumbling out. An odor of ginger plants, and a mental picture of a time past blossoms. I recall exploring a mountain in Hawaii as a child. With a BB gun in hand I climbed hillsides by grabbing onto roots, vines, or branches. Now I am doing the same thing but with an M-16 rifle, the smell of ginger painting the memory. I come upon a pool in a stream and the smell of the water spiced by mossy rocks. As a child, I'd skinny dip in such places. Now, odors drawing memories, I throw a hand grenade to stun and study the different types of fish.

Radio Operators

I live in a bunker. It is dark, wet, musty, and close. I share the bunker with the company radio operators. Always two, sometimes three.

I don't know my radio operators. A company commander is God. They walk with God, sleep with God, and talk with Him. But God is talking to Himself when he talks to his radio operators. It is that kind of relationship.

They seem like the old hag wives of the tribal chief. They are the only ones in my company who can get on me about things. They give me the men's side, the men's view of what is going on. Most of the men do not talk with God, but they know the radio operators do. It is my radio operators who tell them that I am not God. That's how the Corps keeps bullshitters out of the command position in line units. If a skipper shares his bunker with his radio operators, there is no way the he can bullshit the men for very long.

In the field you need at least one radio operator tied into your company radio frequency and one on the battalion radio frequency. If I have three, one monitors the lead platoon's radio net. My battalion radio man moves freely behind me when we are in the field. As long as he can see me and what I can see, he is pretty much free to do his own thing. The radio man on my company net always walks right behind me and to my right. If I want to talk, I switch my rifle to my left hand and grasp the handset of his radio phone with my right. I don't have to say anything or even look; I just switch my rifle. He knows and has the mike ready when I reach back with my right hand. He is totally loyal to me. He is always there when I reach.

The battalion radio operator is a smooth operator, a real piece of work—man has an opinion on everything. I like that. Battalion is always freaky when we are out on patrol. Sometimes you'd swear that they were getting hit when, in fact, we are. When you first get hit, you think the entire North Vietnamese Army is on you. The last thing I want to do is talk to the battalion when I am getting hit. It is my company that I want to talk to, not the battalion. But those pricks back at battalion always want spot reports. As soon as anything starts, they want a report. I always refuse to talk to them before the fight settles down. It might be only minutes, but everyone in battalion has at least two complete nervous breakdowns. My battalion radio operator soothes them. He had been a salesman back in the world, and he sells battalion the thickest line of bullshit you can imagine. He tells them what he thinks is happening. He has no idea—like the rest of us—but that doesn't stop him.

I get a new radio man who has been a machine gunner. Both of my regular radio operators dislike the machine gunner right from the beginning. Neither says anything directly to the new man because he could probably do them both at the same time, but they tell me all about how he's not right for the crew. The new man is one tough, brave, humping guy, but they're right—he can't talk. His voice is too high, and his diction is poor. You have more than enough trouble understanding one another when shit flies—this guy will only make things worse. The radio operators make me banish the new man. I tell him that I need machine gunners more than radio operators. He looks hurt when I tell him. Being a radio operator is a status job. Charlie thinks so, too. He always tries to shoot the radio operators. Cocksucker knows Marines love to talk.

The radio operators and I are like people in a relationship who, for whatever reason, no longer question why they are with each other. Each knows his place and does not question why they are together. We just get along.

The radio operators are always respectful of me in front of others. They put their lives right in my crazy hands. I listen to them, but I never know them. It is not friendship that we have. I am just their job, and they are doing me as best they can.

Kirby

Kirby is one of the radio operators. He was a dirt farmer from Texas before the war. Like a lot of the young Marines, some of his front teeth are missing. Clarity and a pure, sweet coolness on the radio are his specialties. He has the quickest mouth I've ever heard. That's what you want in a radio man, someone who is quick, clear, and concise.

Kirby is my teacher. I credit him more than anyone with breaking me in right. When I arrive he had already done 9 months. From him I learn what it is that the men want most from their skipper. First and foremost it is to be left alone. I can do whatever I want with the lieutenants under my command, and they in turn control the squad leaders. Each squad is, however, an independent family unit. I am king of the hill, and the men accept that. But I should not interfere with the established internal order. They expect me to tell them when to patrol and where, but other than that they want to be left alone. My job is to ensure that they are taken care of and, more important, to keep the Marine Corps off their backs. Every man there knows exactly how much time he has left to do in Nam and the Corps. Fuck the mickey mouse.

Kirby is wise for his age—19, I think. I wonder if it is the war that has made him wise. Who would need his type of wisdom back in the world?

I love listening to his stories of life down on the farm. When the crop was harvested, he'd get a new pair of shit-kicker boots and a pair of jeans. He tells me about the nest egg—the egg that is left for the hen so she keeps coming back to the same spot. The pinnacle of grossness in Kirby's farm life had been when the nest egg broke on him. It was a very rotten egg. Kirby also teaches me what *becretchit* means. "He was a becretchit old man." Can't you just see the old geezer all wrinkled and hunched over? Becretchit.

I listen so much. Living that close to other men day

in and day out teaches me about listening. A man doesn't talk—not like a woman, anyway. A man talks about who he is or what he's thinking. A woman tells you about every fucking thing that's happened to her that day. Women must like to hear themselves talk.

The Squad

For the Marine rifleman, life is his squad. A squad is supposed to consist of 14 men: a squad leader (a sergeant E-5), a grenadier, and three fire teams of 4 men each. Fire teams are supposed to be led by a corporal E-4. Radio operators are supposed to be supplied by the battalion communications company.

We are so undermanned in Nam that most of our squads consist of only five or six men including the radio operator. Most of the squad leaders are corporals or even lance corporals—E-3s. A new recruit is an E-1.

The Marine squads are led by 18- and 19-year-old kids. If a Marine lasts 3 months in combat, he can become a squad leader. A guy can be a nose-picking civilian one day and, if he is lucky, a squad leader in combat 6 months after joining the Corps. An old-man squad leader is 21 years old. The squad leader is usually the one with the longest time in the squad.

It is up to the squad leader to ensure that all his men are effective riflemen. Squads live together, literally. A squad leader is either tight with his men or he is meat. If his men turn on him, he is dead. Some of the squad leaders are the skinniest little fuckers imaginable. They have teeth missing and are the ugliest creatures a woman could give birth to. These little fuckers can tell a big black dude from Detroit what to do, and the dude does it. All this by the time a squad leader is 19. Toughest man leads in the Marines—size has nothing to do with it. Some of the guys would turn down a chance at being squad leader. They knew that they didn't have it.

Most squads have initiation ceremonies in which the fantasies of the squad leader are played out with all members participating. One of my lieutenants tells me about one squad's ritual. First the new man has to jerk off in front of the squad members to prove his manhood. Then all the squad members pack the guy's crotch in mud.

A new man is thrown right into a line unit. He leaves the States on a jet and in less than 48 hours he finds himself out on an ambush with real live ammunition. If he hits it right, he can be a salty-ass veteran in less than a week.

The men of the squad do the fighting. Once fighting starts, talking stops. Squad leaders take over. There is none of this time-out shit and no huddle or talking to the coach on the sidelines. You kill what is trying to kill you or you are dead. I operate in free-fire zones. What you see, you shoot.

We get so short of men sometimes that the squad leader has to carry the radio as well as the grenade launcher. He is a true macho man. Squad leaders even take their turn walking point, or being the man in front when the squad is on patrol. The squad leaders serve as an example. That's what Marines believe in: Don't tell me, motherfucker, show me.

An officer needs to stay out of the squad's way as much as possible. That squad humps all day out in the bush. When we stop for the night, they spend an hour or more digging in. That night they pull an ambush patrol and are up from midnight until 4:00 or 5:00 in the morning—this after being on 50 percent alert before going out. We all start humping and searching for Charlie again at first light.

Outward Bound, my ass! A 19-year-old squad leader who puts himself and his men through that day after day, 7 days a week, gets old real fast. He gets set in his ways and does not like any bullshit. His job is a hassle. Worrying about other peoples' lives is a fucking hassle.

Lifers

I've always disliked lifers, and lifers have always controlled the Marine Corps. Maybe that's the definition of institutionalization: Those in power become lifers.

Institutionalization. That's what lifers are all about. They have to have an institution to exist. Their drive to institutionalize is probably based in their desire to belong. They need a creed, a set of rules, or a bible to guide them. Lifers do not exist outside their institutions. They shape themselves into some mold, and as time goes on the original purpose of the conformity loses significance. Form instead of content. Symbols instead of meaning.

Supply Guys

As supply sergeant, Delta Company has one of the smoothest operators around. He is a black dude, a sergeant E-5. Supply is about juice—power—and this guy has it. Good supply guys are wheeler-dealers, and this dude can deal. If I would just let him go down to Da Nang, he claims, he could get me a tank.

"What the fuck am I going to do with a tank, and just how the fuck do you propose getting it here?"

He just smiles his big gold-toothed smile. "I got connections in this man's Marine Corps, yes suh."

George is his name, and what a storyteller he is. We sit around late at night, my lieutenants and I, listening in awe to his stories. His life has been the greatest adventure.

Once, when he was on a Mediterranean tour, he went to Morocco on leave. Bought himself a slave girl, he claims. "It was always my dream to see firsthand what slavery was about." He roars his deep baritone laugh.

According to his story, she was beautiful, of course, and soon fell madly in love with him. We all laugh so hard that no one ever dreams of telling George that he is full of shit. What a con man he is.

He loves to eat, so we feed him from our care packages. One of his favorite treats is sardines and crackers thick with hot sauce. Hot food just adds a fire to his eyes as he tells his tales. We drink cup after cup of instant coffee cooked over a field stove while listening. His tales of life as a Marine are not what we know. One of his stories is about his R&R in Thailand.

During his first day in Bangkok he discovered that you could exchange whores. "If you got to the club before 11:00 p.m., you could turn 'em back and get another one." George would wait for the club to open and see how many girls he could do before 11:00. With his eyes lit up, he tells the story just like Cinderella doing a countdown. "Girl be saying 'No, no, he fuck me plenty times' to the momma san," he chuckles.

Funny thing about George, he always wears a helmet.

I don't think I ever see him without it on. Even when there isn't anything happening, George always wears his helmet.

Corpsmen

How can you not admire them? Those that stay in the field with us, anyway. We do not keep corpsmen with an attitude problem. Fuck no, we ship them right back to battalion medical. God bless the battalion surgeon. He never tolerates any chicken-shit squid corpsmen like those fat-assed cocksuckers that you saw so often back in the world.

Every platoon has a corpsman, and the men treat him more like a mascot. Everyone takes care of him because when show time comes, it is the corpsman who is expected to get up and move to whomever is down. Corpsmen do it, too. They get up and move under fire time after time.

Some of the bravest guys I see are corpsmen. A lot of them seem to have an inner power. Not having the burden of having to kill but of having to save seems to make them stronger than we are. I even see corpsmen gently work on NVAs that we wound. I have to hold some of my guys back from killing the gooks while the corpsman works on them. Our job is to kill; his is to save. God is everywhere.

The Chaplain

Most chaplains come and go—I can't keep them straight. Various religious types come out to the hills to do masses or whatever, but one chaplain is there from the time I arrive. He reminds me of Goofy, the cartoon character. He is the only chaplain I ever see go out on patrol.

I am sitting in a bomb crater on Hill 881 with this chaplain. He keeps going on about how he is not allowed to be armed. "All I can carry are these little pencil flares," he says. "I'm going to defend myself with these pencil flares?" Khe Sanh can do that to you; God has lost a hold of that boy's ass. The chaplain is doing his own thing.

The man is hooked on cocoa. He drinks it all the time. Cocoa is hard to come by—not that many packets of it are in a case of C rations. Chaplain always raids the cocoa and the cookies, too, because chocolate comes with the cookies—with the vanilla cremes. He comes out to the hills and steals our fucking chocolate. What are you going to say? He is selling insurance, and a lot of guys are cashing in on policies. So you don't want any guy badmouthing your ass with God.

He does make me laugh. I don't think he ever talks religion with me. He always has stories about what he's been up to, like living in a native village. "It's just like being a *National Geographic* researcher!" he exclaims. Excitedly he does a *National Geographic* commentary for me. His eyes are like movie projectors blinking in a dark theater. He is all animated. Chaplain lives in the past all the time. He never talks future. I guess not many of us do.

Boots

Jungle boots are the first truly practical, comfortable thing I get in Vietnam. I do a lot of humping in my first pair. I wear holes in the nylon sides. That is a mark of distinction, to wear out your boots like that. They have black leather toes and heels. Mine are worn to a smooth, almost creamy luster from constant rubbing against dirt, branches, rocks, logs, rain, streams, heat, sweat, and piss. Those suckers form perfectly to my feet. My feet go into my boots like a perfect fit with pussy. I am real tight with those boots.

Protective Gear

The helmets of Marines and the helmets of doggies (the U.S. Army) are different. Doggies' helmet covers have a different camouflage design, and they always look new. Doggie officers must make their men change helmet covers every time they get dirty. Marines from Khe Sanh have reddish covers because Khe Sanh dirt is a distinctive red. Doggies wear chin straps that split under the chin. Our air officer and one of the artillery observers wear those straps, and they look like doggies. Field Marines do not wear chin straps. We fasten the strap on the back of our helmets.

The steel helmet has a fiberglass liner inside that is removable. The liner has an inner adjustable leather band that fits like a headband—that's what holds the helmet on your head. You'd give yourself a headache adjusting a new liner to your head.

We call our helmets piss pots. You can wash or even shit in a helmet. I watch ARVNs (soldiers of the Army of the Republic of Vietnam, the South Vietnamese) cook rice in theirs.

Marines have started a rumor that in a blast a man with his chin strap on could have his head torn off. After what I see at Khe Sanh, I'd say that any blast could do that; if it gets your chin strap, it probably gets the rest of your raggedy ass, too.

How do Marines keep their helmets on when they dive for cover? Left hand. The left hand goes up and holds the helmet on. Right hand? Lots of guys break their fall with their right hand. But most blacks, and myself, and a few other guys cover the jewels. Right hand goes over the nuts.

If rockets come in when I am in the open, I dive into the nearest trench with my left on the helmet and my right over my nuts. I believe in protecting the most important parts. Rockets can have an arm or leg, but not my balls. I'd kill myself if I lost them. Guys who put their right hand down that way would all do suicides if they lost the nuts.

We even have flak pants. You wear them like a pair of boxer shorts. Guys who wear them get razzed to shit. I know one guy who wears them all the time. He doesn't give a fuck what anyone says. He's giving his nuts every chance that he can.

Superstition—Another Protection

"Here, Skipper. I'm leaving, and it's brought me luck," the young Marine says as he stops at my bunker to say goodbye. He offers me a rabbit's foot—one of those things about an inch and a half long with a little chain hooked to one end. It had probably been white at one time; now it looks like a small brown turd.

I hook it to the ring of my Swiss army knife. Boy, does that thing stink. It finally just rots away.

Issue .45

Image

I enjoy listening to other people talking about what they think their physical shortcomings are. I think with women it's their tits. You know, they're never right. Too big, too small, too elongated—whatever. I remember I knew a woman once who kept asking me if I thought her tits were all right. I said, "Shit, baby, they look fine to me." You know what she thought was wrong? Her nipples didn't point straight out, they pointed slightly to the sides. You had to look to notice. I mean, how technical do you have to get?

There seem to be a lot of short Marines. My first three platoon commanders are short. In fact, one is nick-named Short Round. I'm taller than average for a Marine—5 feet 11 inches. But being nearly blind and having to wear glasses does not help my image. It is a strike against you as an officer if you wear glasses. The Corps doesn't help, either. They give me glasses that make me look even more ridiculous than civilian glasses do. Military issue is gray, shatterproof, and stupid looking.

The first week that I'm on 861, I break the first of the several pairs I have with me. I am cleaning my pistol one morning, and I don't hold the slide firmly. The spring pops free and hits me in the left lens, shattering my supposedly shatterproof glasses. Like an idiot, I have a corpsman check my eye out. Nothing's wrong with my eye, but the bigmouth tells how I screwed up, and soon I'm the newest ha-ha on the hill. I don't want a bumbling-fool reputation and decide I will change that image the first chance I get. I'm not pissed at anyone, and I understand perfectly what those men might be thinking. Marines follow; they don't mind being led. But they sure as shit don't want a wet-dream leading them. They don't like suck-ass lifers, but they like jerk-offs even less.

There is a squad test-firing their weapons one day on Hill 861. They stand at the wire in front of the trench. A deep gully runs along the west side of 861. They are shooting down into the gully and out across at a ridgeline a couple of hundred yards away.

When you are out in the field on your own, you can fire off whatever you want whenever you want; you don't have to go through all the shit that they make you go through back in the world. Back in the world, they were so uptight about anyone getting hurt that they made you do elaborate safety bullshit before you ever fired a shot. "Ready on the right, ready on the left, all ready on the firing line," some asshole would say. Firing in combat is not like that. No one asks if you are ready or not. If you aren't ready, you are dead. Pure and simple.

I pick up an M-79, a 40mm grenade launcher. After I load a round I casually aim off into the gully. Cool, just cool, you know? I pull the trigger. Tonk! The grenade launcher makes a rather quiet sound—we call it a Tonk gun. But I hadn't noticed a branch about 30 feet in front of me. The round hits the branch and explodes. Guys go down, dive down, squat down. I'm shocked.

I look around and everyone's eyes are on me. Eyes, undecided eyes. I reach down, pick out another round, pop the empty shell, chamber the new round, and snap the chamber shut. I raise the weapon, aim one handed, and fire. Tonk! I deliberately hit the tree again. I'm the only one standing. Everyone's got an I-don't-believe-this-guy look on their faces. I say casually, "Blast only goes straight forward when you hit like that."

I'm lying my ass off, but I'll be damned if I'm going to be punching out my glasses again in front of these suckers. That's one thing about me, I learn quick. Macho is about quickness. I turn a fuck-up right around and achieve two things: I make them doubt I'm a goof, a klutz, or an idiot, and—more important—they are not sure if I am crazy or reckless or what. I've ceased to be a ha-ha, a joke's-on-me-type guy.

Moving

Do you know what triple canopy means? Most of the terrain around Khe Sanh is triple-canopy jungle. It starts with a ground layer of plants or shrub brush. A layer of low trees or tall bushes make the second layer, then tall trees provide the top layer. That's the essence of jungle. Not the vines and snakes slithering around. Not some guy howling and swinging through the trees on a vine. Just a thick growth of grasses, plants, and trees all around you.

When you look around you in the jungle, you have no idea where the fuck you are. Even though I faithfully follow my map and continually check, that ol' feeling is eating at me. Somehow, when I am deep in the bush, I swear I am lost. I trust myself rationally, but deep inside something is saying, you're lost, asshole. You're fucking lost. You took a wrong turn somewhere, and you're lost. I let out a sigh of relief every time I walk out of the jungle into an open area where I can see again. The jungle is like that.

On one patrol I go for three full days of that doubt. Three days moving in thick jungle where I can't see the sky except for brief moments. On other patrols I'd confirm my position by taking compass readings off known terrain features. I'd usually use a hill that I recognized. But this time I can't see anything to take compass readings on, and since no one had ever really surveyed the area, the map is not always right. I use streams and how the streams cross trails as reference points. At times I have one of our artillery or mortar spotters climb a tree to try to get readings. Our artillery is supposed to be accurately registered, so sometimes we have them fire near us, and we take sound sightings with our compasses. You have to know where you are if you want to get help.

The feeling of being lost bugs the shit out of me. I hate not knowing. But location is not the biggest problem in the jungle; moving is.

There is only one way that you can move effectively in jungle: You move in column. One asshole behind the other in file and in line, like a centipede weaving through the jungle. That's what we are—a hundred guys or so, 200 legs moving like a centipede.

I get pissed off when the battalion asks why we are moving so slowly. The battalion operations officer tries to tell me how and where to go. I think about him and the rest of the guys back at the battalion command post. Sitting in their bunker, all they have to do is look at a map on the wall. That's what they're doing while we are out there scraping leeches off our asses. Life's a bitch when you're smoking a cigarette, drinking coffee, and waiting for someone to move an inch or two on the map. They pimp me a lot.

You are supposed to radio your position every 30 minutes so they can track you. On one patrol I move less than 1,000 meters in one whole day. They do not believe me. I know that the guys back at battalion just cannot understand how thick it is. You know what I do the next day? I move like a motherfucker. At least that's what they think back at the battalion. Every 30 minutes I report back a new position. I jump all over that map of theirs. I'm not going anywhere, but they think I am. At the end of the day the colonel tells me over the radio, "Great patrolling, Delta 6." How the hell do they know? It is like they are trying to share the moment with me. Except what they think happened and what actually happened are two different things.

I'm lucky—I never get hit when I do that. I do it a number of times, too. I always try to let them know if they are full of shit about how to work an area, but if they keep insisting, I pretend I'm doing it their way. There are times when they tell me to go over a cliff even though the close contour lines on the map mean steep, real steep. I say, "Sure, right," then I go around my way. I figure if they ever find out, what are they going to do? Send me to Vietnam?

I remember seeing an army airborne unit on a sweep. The battalion commander has his own helicopter fly just above the troops. Man, I don't think I could take some cocksucker hovering over me like that, ragging at me about my every move. Motherfucker would have taken fire every time he got over me. My fire.

Hands

When I am out in the bush, I use my left hand to tell other people what to do, how to go, and what to hit. My right hand is all mine.

Me and my right hand go way back. It fed me. It put the cigarette to my mouth and touched my lips as it did so. Every guy I ever dropped with one hand dropped from a punch from my right. I tried smoking with my left hand, but it never felt as good. Same with jerking off, wiping my ass, and tying my boots. It just never felt correct—it never felt right.

Out in the bush my right hand is on its own as much as possible. That fucker is like one of those sharp-ass hyper hunting dogs. Turn, point, tense, untense. When my right hand is near something that smells like NVA, it tenses my whole arm up.

There are three ways that I hold an M-16. If there is little danger, I hold my rifle barrel up, right elbow against my side, and right palm rotated toward my face. This is the most comfortable way to walk while still being ready to fire. It is a hard position to get off from quickly, though. Holding the tip of the rifle downward with the right hand

and letting the right arm swing free lets me shoot faster. When Charlie is close and I am as cocked as the rifle, only one grip will do: I hold the M-16 with the top pointing forward, the right elbow tucked along my side, the palm outside the firing guard, and my right index finger on the trigger. When my finger is inside the trigger guard, it is show time and my right hand almost vibrates. I talk to it and remind it to pull. In this position I am just a finger pull away from turning someone into a Christmas tree.

My right hand is the way I want to be: free to unload on someone.

Packing

Ammo requirements for a six-day long-range patrol are set, but each man can pack as much food as he is willing to carry. Some of the boys like to eat, too. There is one fool who straps two packs together, one with nothing but chow in it.

I smoke Salems, and I carry them in my right trouser pocket. Big pockets that run halfway down the thighs of my jungle utilities. You can pack a lot of shit in one of those pockets. I put my poncho in the left one. In the right pocket I put cigarettes, matches, and maps.

All things are done for a purpose: I am right-handed, and I put the stuff where the right hand can get at it. My poncho is in my left pocket because that is the side I will fall to if I go down. If we are hit, I will go down on my left side so I can either shoot or go for my map. I remind myself of that every time I pull my poncho from my left pocket.

I use one of the new lightweight packs. It is feather

light when empty and can carry twice as much as the standard Marine Corps issue. I love to eat, and I load that son of a bitch with all kinds of C rations. It's Chow City for this kid.

As much as possible I try to keep everything packed in back or on the back of my web belt. On my belt are two canteens, an ammo packet that holds four clips, a compass case, and my dearest treasure—the first-aid kit. In the kit are my Swiss army knife, Merthiolate, and battle dressings. Battle dressings come in individual packets. They are like sanitary napkins with long gauze ribbons at each end for tying. You never want to get on the rag in Nam. You might never get off.

Except for the ammo pouch on my right front and the first-aid kit on the left, I keep my front clear. Clear to go down. Low. Bullets move in straight lines. If you can somehow get your ass beneath Charlie's line of sight, he will not be able to hit you. Any man who doesn't give himself every break he can is either stupid or one of those medal chasers. I am neither. I am a low motherfucker. I was 5 feet 11 inches when I arrived, but after a while I start shrinking. I feel like I am melting right down into my boots.

Carrying

I carry a rifle in the field. I know I'm not supposed to, but I always carry in the field. An officer is supposed to carry just a pistol. Pistol, my ass. If I'm going to shoot, I'm going to get some. Using a pistol in a fire fight is like trying to get pussy from across the street. Dream on, motherfucker. I carry real heat in the field. M-16, shot-

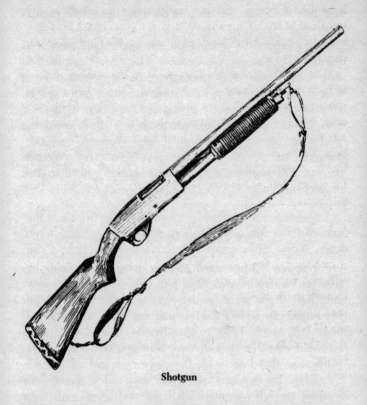

Shotgun

gun, or grease gun. Fuck 'em, I'm the one who's out there, they aren't.

You can say what you want about the M-16 rifle. It does jam a lot in fire fights, but it can also put out some heat in a hurry. If you want to light some guy up, there is no better way than with an M-16. It fires so quickly, the guy is dead before he hits the ground. AK-47s (Charlie's rifle) and our M-60 machine guns knock guys around and tear them up. M-16s just do 'em. Instant Christmas tree.

I'm sure most women do not understand why it is that guys like to carry a weapon. The closest comparison that I can think of is pregnancy. Being pregnant for a woman is similar to a guy carrying. A woman gets a special kind of alive when she's pregnant. I can see it in their eyes. A man carrying looks the same way. Both are doing everything they can to protect life. Women "carrying" seem to last longer than the guys who carry. Women protect and nurture their babies; "babies" nurture and protect their men.

Slow Dancer in Rock City

I am an old-fashioned Marine. I believe in firing my rifle on semiautomatic. One pull of the trigger gets you one shot. If you want another, you pull the trigger again. My finger can go like a scratching dog doing a bad case of fleas. It is quick. I like to aim, too. My preferences make me what we call a slow dancer. Now you take some of the youngsters that I am with, they love rock and roll.

Elvis Presley, my ass. Rock and roll is firing your weapon on full automatic. All the way over with your selector switch—the process is called busting caps. The selector switch is like a big toothpick that sits on the left side of the rifle just above the trigger guard. If you are right-handed, you can move the switch with your right thumb and still keep your trigger finger on the trigger. I swear the black dudes weld their selector switches on rock and roll.

If you want to get some, one of the best ways is on

rock and roll. Rock and roll is especially handy just after you get ambushed and can't see.

I hear that the Marine Corps might put a restrictor on M-16 rifles to keep a guy from dumping the full clip of ammo at once. Those restricted firing mechanisms are going to last about 2 weeks in combat. The Marines who are left after that 2 weeks will saw them off. Rock and roll is here to stay!

Going Out on Patrol

There is a ritual I always go through before I go out on patrol. I check all my equipment beforehand, but when I step outside the wire, I always check my piece (my rifle). Whatever it is that I am carrying, I check it; I touch and feel my piece. I think about what I am carrying and what it can do. You shift gears in your head when you go out beyond the wire. You are turned all the way on—every switch you have is on when you go out. Time after time, I patrol all around. Farther and farther out, for longer and longer periods. Even when I'm not getting hit, I'm on. I never have any trouble staying jacked up when I'm out in the bush.

You see so much when you are that way—jacked up like that. Every move is a recomputed checklist. You're constantly going over items with yourself. You are constantly looking over the terrain. Your eyes and head turn in the rhythms of your body movement. You pick out where you'll go or move if you're hit. You're recalculating how you'll react if fire comes from various points out in front or from the sides. You just take it all in. Knowing.

This is what is always going on in my head when I am

out in the bush and in command. Every time. Even when the beauty is all around me. My eyes see the beauty, but I stay jacked up. I have that much respect for what is happening. I am always ready for it to go off. The passage of time does not do anything to lessen that feeling. That up feeling is walking right along on the edge. Every step is life. Everything is so fucking real.

I see Marines, my Marines, in front. I look behind. I do that sometimes just to reaffirm that I'm not dreaming. That is the only break in my concentration: wondering if it is for real, since it feels so strong, so real.

My eyes dominate a sense of complete awareness. Not my eyes but an eye. I am one eye. An eye that not only sees, but hears, smells, tastes, and feels. I become one eye when I am moving through the bush. I am aware only of being an eye moving. Looking. My mind and body— everything is one. My awareness is centered. I am completely focused on where I am. All my experiences up to the moment mean nothing except as they relate to my reactions at the moment. I am always cocked and ready to go off.

I always feel that we will be hit first. Every time I am out moving in the bush it is with the feeling that we'll never get off first. In boxing there's a saying that—all things being equal—if you get off first, you win. If we're hit, I know we have to hit back hard. Punch, that's what I always keep telling myself. When they throw, throw back, shoot back, hit back, make your men hit back. Dump on 'em. Burn 'em. Light 'em up!

Down a Trail

We have been out several days, working across very thick jungle and steep terrain. There is no sign of Charlie. We are supposed to sweep the area by zigzagging across it. We can't zigzag—it's too thick. A major NVA supply trail runs through the area we are working. "Fuck it," I finally say. "Get on the trail."

I know that any asshole who comes through here uses the trail. No one, unless he is as stupid as we are, comes through without using the trail. I know Charlie isn't as stupid as we are. If I want to meet him, I have to get on the trail. I know some of the guys brag about how smart they are: They never go on trails and they never get hit. Yeah, and they never hit anything, either.

It is like the haunted house you'd go through when you were a kid. You know that with every step something terrifying can happen. Moving down a trail in the jungle gives me that feeling. Except I know that Charlie is not just going to just jump out from behind a tree and say *boo*. You would probably never see him if he got you. If you were the first to get it, you wouldn't even know what was happening until after you'd been had. I think if you were head shot, you wouldn't even know anything at all. It would be just like a radio turned off in the middle of a note. Boom! Just like that, you'd be gone.

We move on a trail that meanders along a low ridgeline in heavy jungle. I am close to where the trail runs down into a narrow ravine. I am up front with the lead platoon. The point has just crossed a stream at the bottom of the ravine when we hear firing. Not close to me. I think it is coming from up front—echoes in the ravine confuse me. I charge straight down into the stream. More shots are

Water Buffalo

fired, and I realize it's behind me—from back up the trail. Fucking asshole, I think. I turn and race back up the trail. A machine gun fires. Marines are scattered in prone positions beside the trail, tense looks in their eyes. Everyone gets big eyes at such times.

As I near the top of the ridge, I see water buffalo off to my right. They're charging, snorting, and crashing about in the thick brush just off the trail. I dump a full clip into the one coming at me. All semiautomatic tight shots right into the chest. Fucker just stops, shakes his ass, and ambles off as though nothing had happened. On the trail I see a dead water buffalo.

Next to a tree the lieutenant from the rear platoon is down on his back. This is a new lieutenant, and he gets taken out by a fucking water buffalo! It is his first time out, too. How's he going to tell his kids about this? Not only that, but he never fired a shot. The water buffalo had butted him against the tree and repeatedly butted him. The lieutenant couldn't do a thing. He had yelled for his radio operator to shoot, but his operator, Pee Wee, just jumped from side to side trying to decide what to do. Finally, a machine gunner took the buffalo out with a long burst from his M-60.

When I get there a skinny little Marine is trying to cut the tail off the dead water buffalo.

"What the fuck are you doing, son?" I ask.

"I dunno, Skipper, I thought it would look kinda neat carrying it as a souvenir."

"This ain't a fucking safari. Get rid of it."

A corpsman slits the trousers on the lieutenant's injured leg.

"Well, what's it going to be?" I ask.

"We'll have to get him medevaced, Skipper."

Taking the handset from my battalion radio operator, I transmit, "Blackbud, this is Blackbud Delta. Over."

"Delta, this is Blackbud. Go ahead," comes the immediate reply.

"We're going to need a dustoff. We ran into some wild water buffalo, and I got one man badly dinged. Over."

"Roger, Delta, did you say that was water buffalo? Over."

Before I can answer, another transmission comes over the radio.

"Blackbud Delta, this is Blackbud 3 actual. Let me have Delta 6 actual. Over." I recognize the voice of the assistant operations officer. He is a suck-ass lifer prick.

"You got him, 3," I sass.

"Delta 6, what's going on out there? I want a full report."

"You'll get it, 3, as soon as I get back. Now how about my dustoff."

Next I recognize the colonel's voice on the radio. In his quiet drawl he says, "Uh, Delta 6, what's going on? Over."

"What can I say? We crossed with a herd of wild water buffalo. We killed one, and I shot one myself. We got a guy down. Over."

"OK, Delta 6, but please be careful out there. This is Blackbud 6. Out."

Careful shit, I think to myself. Like we egged the fuckers on?

We find a spot down near the stream for a landing zone, and I have the lieutenant carried there. We frantically clear a patch for the helicopter. Do you know what the lieutenant's little shit radio operator does after all that? The lieutenant is lying there waiting to get lifted out, and Pee Wee eases on up to him.

"Hey, Lieutenant, can I have your chow?"

If I had been that lieutenant, I would have had double ass that day—buffalo and radio operator. At that point, though, I am going after my own ass. I don't like the fact that I misjudged where the shots came from.

Incoming rifle fire takes learning. All your training is with outgoing. In training, you shoot. Shootings are always forward, in front of you. Incoming, that's different, all the way different.

The Difference

There is a whole world of difference between outgoing and incoming fire. Outgoing can seduce you. The first thing you notice is the sound. When watching and listening to outgoing, girls scream and guys get hard-ons.

Incoming makes you understand what is really happening in a war. War is about killing your ass. That ol' light goes right on even in the thickest of skulls. Bingo! You get the true picture real quick with incoming. The sound of a rifle going off when you shoot it ain't shit. Try standing in front of it, and you'll understand, especially when you realize that you're not standing in front of William Tell and there's no apple on your head. You think you've heard cannon fire? Try sitting in the middle of the explosion. Sound. It's all in the difference in the sound. Yep, firing is about killing, and you're it with incoming.

The First Time

The first time I think we are getting hit is on Hill 861 a few weeks after I get there. We have an LP (a listening post) out beyond the wire on the top of the hill. The LP is next to a trail running through a bamboo thicket that grows to within 30 feet of our wire. The LP reports movement on both sides of their position. It is just after 1:00 in the morning. The radio operator monitoring the network wakes me. I dress quickly and go outside. I walk to the top of the hill over a slight rise. We are fogged in. I can't see the wire I know to be only 40 feet in front of me. I can hear the ground crunch under my boots as I walk back to my bunker. Maybe I am just showing off to myself, but I am unarmed. I am not carrying. I do not feel anything close.

We fire 60mm mortars around the LP for about 30 minutes. The lieutenant at that sector reports that he's taken two grenades right in front of him. Wait a minute, I think, the 60mm mortars are firing in pairs. The heat the lieutenant's taking is probably our own. I feel it is a false alarm. I have them shut down the mortars. I tell the lieutenant to hold fire. I tell my radio operator to bullshit battalion while I go to talk with the LP.

Their nostrils spouting steam, their eyes wide and darting, the men on the listening post have just walked the edge. I might have surmised that it was a false alarm, but they had sure felt death out there. They had heard the noises in the bamboo. But I know it wasn't Charlie. He might be a skinny-assed fucker, but he isn't that thin. Charlie would not go through the bamboo—it is just too thick. Battalion wants to send up a spotter plane and fire artillery. No artillery fire, I tell them. It would be coming right over us. It would be too close, I tell them. I didn't tell them that I think it is a false alarm.

Everything comes so easy and natural. I am smooth. I am tight with myself.

A guy wonders if he can trust himself at a time like that. You always wonder whether you'll choke until you've had that time—that time when you clear up any self-doubt. Nothing happens that night, but everyone is up like something is happening. I am just fine. Cool, fine, clear. I am very comfortable in command.

It is such a relief to come to that understanding with myself. What happened to the poor fuckers who didn't trust themselves? Self-trust is the bottom line. Self-trust and luck.

I am lucky; they leave me alone most of the time. I wonder how different it might be if I did not have the time to do things my way. For the most part, that's how the first half of my tour goes—my way. What evolves is of my own choosing. When one is not victimized or does not perceive himself to be the victim, he is free to come to his own conclusions about himself and how he relates to the events in which he participates. I never feel that anyone is manipulating me during the first half of my tour. I feel in control—not just of my situation, but of myself. I have never gone for such a long period like that. I enjoy it. To have decided to be a certain way, that macho way, and to have it unfurl for me the way I want it to, seduces me.

Only one man challenges me as the new commanding officer of Delta Company. A sergeant in charge of 81mm mortars lets me know right away that he wants to be left alone. He does not want a green-ass new-incountry 1st lieutenant telling him what to do. I let him go about one week without saying anything to him. I want his macho to be ready. Then I talk to him alone. I talk to him in a quiet tone of voice and speak very slowly. Looking him straight in the eye, I say, "This is my hill, Sarge, understand? If you don't, then get your fucking ass on the next chopper out. I'm fucking staying."

I can relieve him of command but don't. I respect arrogant people. I'm arrogant. I tell him that although he's been there a long time and I haven't, it doesn't mean a fucking thing because neither of us has shown the other a damn thing yet. "When shit hits, we'll decide," I tell him. I can admire a defiant man like that sergeant. I am that way myself, very territorial. I give him his territory, and he gives me his respect after that. I don't know if he ever likes me, but he respects me. He never challenges me again.

People wonder why we're different. Guys who lead

Marines in combat are different because we do it. There's no reason why other than the fact that we do it. Why doesn't mean a thing to us. Doing it makes you different. It sets you apart forever from the rest of the world.

KING OF THE HILL

In Command

It is the most isolated fire base ever occupied by Marines in Vietnam. Hill 881 South, my hill, is occupied by not only my company but numerous other attached units under my command. Artillery, mortars, an air support group, and even a CIA long-range radio intercept team are on my hill. One day, a general wants to drop in to visit. He arrives in a Huey (an armed helicopter) without escort and radios for permission to land. Anyone who wants to enter my turf has to call and obtain permission first. It is not just a courtesy; it is a necessity. This is a free-fire area. Anything that moves anywhere around my area of responsibility is fair game; I can order it destroyed. I'm looking out and watching that chopper. I look all around me. I'm thinking, Ernest, you're only 24, and you have more power now than you'll ever have again. Ever again. I thought I despised power, and here I am all sucked up in that feeling.

I clear the general in for his landing. I really like this

general. He often visits me out here. My feelings about authority have changed. I see all men, no matter what their rank, as just men. Never again would I be in awe of anyone's position. I know it is all so relative.

My goals and mission are so clear and outside of myself. Perhaps that's why it is so much easier for me than for others. I have so much to do, watch, care for, think about, know, and live for. Commanding the most northwestern, far-out fire base that there is calls for knowledge. I want to know everything.

Lady 881 South

Viewed from a helicopter my hill can really be appreciated for what it is. A mountaintop bastion ringed like a lady's neck with fine strands of diamonds—barbed wire wet from the morning mist reflecting the sun like sparkling jewels. Hill 881 sits atop a conically shaped ridgeline 881 meters above sea level. In the valleys is lush jungle. The ridges bristle with tall, sharp elephant grass. One ridge runs westerly like a causeway from the base of a short steep rise to 881 herself. Anyone attempting to attack the top of Hill 881 would face extremely steep terrain.

Marines had taken 881 South from Charlie just before I arrived incountry. It is one of the major battles that the Marines have fought in Vietnam to date. Charlie did not give her up easily. And now I hold her for us. And we don't just hold her, we flaunt her.

We cut down all the trees around the top and clear the brush for better vision and fields of fire. And do we ever wire the bitch. I believe in wire. I like all types of

Claymore Mine

barbed wire. We place some just 6 inches above ground in a checkerboard fashion. Charlie would have to do quite a dance to get through that. He'd look like one of those stupid football players running through a tire drill. We also place wire in diagonals chest high around our machine-gun positions.

I love Claymore mines and fugas. Claymores are like pendants strung out from our trenches on strands of green wire. They are like unpolished emeralds the size of a small box. The boxes are filled with pellets and explosives. Fugas is a 55-gallon drum filled with jellied gasoline and explosives. I take care of my lady, dress her in the finest jewelry the Marine Corps has.

She takes care of me, too. I live with and on her a number of times, and she is the best. I love her more than 861 because of where 881 South is. It is surrounded by such incredibly beautiful mountains and valleys.

To the north, a few thousand meters away, sits the big bitch herself—881 North.

I take the first patrol up 881 North since the spring battles. When you sleep with Charlie's lady and then walk up on the big bitch and he's not home or he doesn't want to fight, you do get cocky. I do.

When the weather is good I walk my hill in just my trousers and boots—no shirt, just my dog tags around my neck. They hang on a cheap silverlike chain, the type with little balls joined together. Dog tags look like pool passes. I wear rubber silencers on my dog tags so they don't make any noise. The silencers fit around the outside edges. Every edge you can get, baby. I walk on top of the trenches, jumping between the openings.

Sometimes I stand and look out over my kingdom. What a sight it is when the skies start to clear on a misty day. It is as though the fog has been feeding from the teats of the clouds. The fog retreats right before me. Thick fog slick with moistness rolls back and down into the valleys and canyons around my hill. Then a crack of sunlight starts a panicked flight by the clouds. Mountaintops and ridges appear and change their shades of green in the onrushing sunlight. Shades of shiny emerald to lush, rich, robust aquamarine. All this in a matter of minutes.

You breathe differently as you dry out in the sunlight. The air seems to like it better in the sun. Sunshine is a rare treat during the monsoon season. When the sun comes out, one of the men tears open the canvas door to my bunker and shouts, "Sun's comin', Skipper!" My men know how much I enjoy the sunlight. It is like the mailman or Santa Claus has just arrived. I get my smokes and go over to the gunnery sergeant's bunker. Gunny always has a pot of hobo coffee brewed, no matter what the time of day. Hobo coffee is coffee grounds boiled in water without filters—you have to let it settle before you drink it. I take a cup of brew and go sit on top of my bunker, which is at the highest point on the hill. While sitting with my feet dangling over the side, sipping strong black coffee and smoking a cigarette, I watch my kingdom appear. Disneyland doesn't come close.

Men come up out of their bunkers and from the trenches. They look like scroungy, skinny dogs all wet from the night. They are scratching, coughing, farting, and pissing in front of the trenches. Guys go through a ritual like that when the sun feels good.

Gazing out over the mountains, valleys, and ridges—it is mine. We are all alone out here in my kingdom. No other manned positions can see us. When you're king of the hill, you are alone. Answering only to yourself sets you apart. I am all alone.

When you live with killers on some lonesome mountaintop out beyond nowhere and you're The Man, you do adjust. When you pull it off so it seems like it's the most natural thing in the world, then you've adjusted. But it's like taking a big gulp of air and being afraid to exhale. You just keep sucking in and sucking in your personal feelings. I am such a wise fucker doing what I have to do to make it through.

By now I'm actually a captain—well, yes and no. According to the Marine Corps, I make captain July 1,

71

LAW

1967. The Marine Corps just doesn't get around to telling me or anyone else until April 1968. That's how fucked up it is. They have great weaponry. They have telescopes that can see in the dark. They have elaborate listening devices that can hear gooks fart out in the bush. But it takes 9 months for the Marines to let me or my battalion know that I am promoted. So I'm the only 1st lieutenant commanding a rifle company in our regiment. Most captains in Nam only get 4 or 5 months with a rifle company. The stress is considered too great to do more. As a 1st lieutenant, I command Delta Company for almost 8 months.

I can handle myself. One day the weapons squad is practicing and test-firing LAWs. A LAW is a Light Anti-tank Weapon—a one-shot collapsible rocket launcher. A small rocket crater across on a ridgeline is their target. As I walk by, the squad leader challenges me. "You want in on the contest, Skipper?" he asks. After opening a LAW, I hold it up and just point it above the pockmark they are trying to hit. It is far beyond the effective range of the rocket launcher. Boom! The blast sends a cloud of dust up around me. I watch the round, a black arch, reach high out and over the ravine, then fall like an arrow and explode in the center of the target crater. A loud cheer goes up. After casually dropping the spent cannister, I begin walking away.

A short, dirty southern boy asks me how I had aimed it. "Hey, what kinda windage was you using, Skipper?"

"Kentucky," I answer back over my shoulder. The term *Kentucky windage* refers to flintlock rifles, which had fixed, non-adjustable sights. When a cross wind was blowing you allowed for it with an inspired guess.

A hooting roar and laughter goes up. Not looking

back, I continue my casual strut along the top of the trench line. It was a lucky shot, but a skipper needs a reputation any way he can get it.

Food

Another thing I can't get enough of is food. I hear about all the wonderful things we are supposed to be getting in Vietnam. Things like meat, milk, eggs, and two beers a day per man. We never get much of that at Khe Sanh. The weather is usually so bad that only essentials come in. I eat C rations all the time. We have some eggs, milk a few times, and steaks once.

You really can get into C rations after a while, though. You take joy in what little you have. Eating reminds you every day that you have made it. It is proof that you have made it since your last meal. Eating is like hope.

Eating is a private affair, not a communal thing like it is back in the world. A guy usually eats his own meal alone. You eat when you want to. Time has ceased to have any meaning, so you get into your own rhythms.

A meal is a ritual event. Every time is a special time. Every green can is a little Christmas present to yourself. Julia Child has nothing on us. We mix spices, whatever, to change around what we are eating.

I think about the shit I eat day after day, and I think I must have turned into a dog—one of those scroungy little mutts with its ribs showing. I am one of those anything-tastes-good types of dog. What has happened to my taste buds? Some of the shit I really get into can almost give me a nut sometimes. Like when it is late at night. Outside it's a foggy, wet, cold motherfucker. Inside it's me and a can of beef spiced with sauce over crackers. I put cheese spread and Tabasco sauce on the cracker, then the beef over that. First, though, I heat the beef in the can over heat tabs. Heat tabs look like big blue throat lozenges or a real small bar of soap. The stove is an empty cracker can crimped at the top and with air holes cut at the bottom. I put the heat tab at the bottom of the cracker can, and it provides just enough fuel to heat a single can of food. I am like a geisha doing a tea ceremony.

A meal prepared that way with just a kerosene lamp providing the lighting. The joy is not just in eating; it is in the whole quiet moment with yourself. The whole ritual of a meal. You never want to rush it, either. You never know if you can get another one that way or ever again. When the mood and circumstances are right, it is almost pussy. The meal would not be as good if I didn't realize that it could be the last. When it feels that way, food tastes so sumptuous.

Back in the world I would not eat beef spiced with sauce. It is dog shit. The canned cheese spread is just awful, in point of fact. How one's perspective does change.

Mail

The only thing you really have besides chow is mail. Mail causes mixed emotions for me. My wife writes every day. I mean every day. She sends me a package every week. I know whether the Marine Corps is screwing up by how my mail and packages do or do not come in. I wonder how many other motherfuckers my wife is feeding from the packages I don't receive.

Mail is a mixed blessing because it takes me back to

the world. The world has become so unreal to me. My mail is like a movie, a vision, a fleeting glance, a faded memory. The situation, the place I am in now, demands my emotions, my being, my total attention. It is that kind of place, that kind of life. As you watch a guy reading his mail, it is as though he is a million miles away. I think mail is the thing that comes closest to taking a guy out of the war for a minute or two. Mail is about hopes and dreams. Nam is about reality.

I feel sorry for guys who don't get mail. Believe it? There are some guys who don't get any mail. That is a lonely man. You are alone in Nam, but to be alone back in the world, too? Man, that's lonesome. I am a spoiled brat. Women always spoil me. My wife writes every day. I'm not tough, she is. We are dreamers, both of us.

The Power of the Word

Chow and mail are escapes. Swearing is a tool. It's amazing how powerful swearing is. I know from experience that I've had some people close to fainting from some of my better routines. *Fuck* is the one word all the guys from all over the country have in common. We build off it and develop our own expressive language. Swearing is the most genteel thing we know how to do. People should realize that it is difficult for us salty Marines not to swear. We really do try and watch our language as much as possible, especially when there's cunt present.

Swearing is an insult. War is an insult. It all goes together. We are violent men who practice violence like a game. Swearing is an essential part of our brotherhood. It sets us apart from the world, which has set itself apart from us. Fuck 'em, you know? It is like taking a shot, striking out without hurting anyone.

The best lessons, however, are given with the fewest words. On Hill 881 South in the middle of the day, I am walking the trench line as I do every day. I look around, and no matter where I look, I can't see another Marine. No sentries. No firing positions manned. Nothing. I'll grant you that during the day the trench line is lightly manned. At least one platoon is out on patrol, and most of the guys are still sleeping because they work every night on ambushes and listening posts. Days are supposed to be casual, but not this casual. I pick up an M-16 rifle and climb on top of a bunker. After flipping the selector switch onto semiautomatic, I shoot everywhere. All over the place. Just like in one of those gangster movies. I do one clip of 20 shots real fast. Guys start popping out of holes and bunkers just like prairie dogs. I stand there on top of the bunker looking out across the hill with my rifle at my side, legs apart, and a deep, heavy motherfucker look on my face. My head doesn't move, just my eyes. My eyes move back and forth, back and forth. I wait there silently until they come up out of their holes and bunkers. Sheepishly they come slinking out of their holes as only Marines can be sheepish when they're caught fucking up. With one even motion, I throw the rifle out to my side, jump down off the bunker, and walk away. I do not miss stride. I look straight ahead and say nothing. But God was talking. He didn't have to say a word. They all heard me.

Getting Nasty

At one point the Corps tries to beef up security on the hills by bringing in guard dogs. A dog handler brings a huge German shepherd up to my hill. He thinks he and his dog are King Shit.

"Stay away from this dog," he tells me pompously. "He's a killer."

He builds the mutt a better hootch than some of my men live in. He wires off a large area where the dog can play.

Ol' Killer does not like to patrol, however. He loses his nuts somewhere outside the wire. Fido does patrol two times, then flat refuses to go.

"It's the wet," the handler tells me. "He can't stand all the wetness."

"Great!" I say. "We'll send for the two of you the next time we invade Arizona. Now why don't you and The Killer get the fuck off my hill. And clean up the dog shit before you go, spunky."

That dog is no fool. Imagine being soaking, fucking wet all day and all night long. Cold mountain wet. Going for a week of that. Eating cold food out of cans real quick so that the rain doesn't get to it first. Chow's the only thing you look forward to all day, and you have to tear through it like that.

Imagine going for day after day climbing up and down canyons, switching from humping through sharp, cutting elephant grass to thick jungle. The wind can really whip at your ass through the elephant grass. Rain drives horizontally at you when you crest a ridgeline. The wind, rain, and cold drive right through you.

Then you drop almost straight down into a deep

canyon or ravine. Halfway down you hit heavy jungle again. Thick jungle lines the canyon all the way to the bottom. Constant tapping, plunking sounds on the helmet from the large droplets that gather on the thick, big-leafed plants. The inevitable stream at the bottom. Leeches waiting to jump out from behind a bush and right through the fly of your trousers. Right on and up inside your dick. Before you can react it would climb right in your pisser. Holy shit, the ultimate fucking nightmare. The leech would swell up in your dick on your own blood. You'd get a permanent hard-on from the inside. The leech would die in there, and you'd never be able to get it out.

Lying there shaking from the cold in your soaking wet clothes, rolled in a wet poncho, you wake dreaming that dream. Water is running over and all around you. I lie there and think to myself, I can't believe that you volunteered for this shit, Ernest. If Charlie is out in this shit, then he is a fool too.

Being that way and feeling that way day after day makes you nasty. We see no signs of Charlie during most of the monsoon season. Being a fool makes you nasty. I am a very nasty fucker.

Sleeping Out

When we are out at night on patrol, I like to put in at out-of-the way places. Most Marines like hilltops. I use them too, if it is in real open country. But when I am deep in the bush, I bivouac in a natural hollow if I can. I like to keep all my men in close and tight. We always dig in, too. Always. We set up so that Charlie has to be real close before he can hit us. I want everyone close so that we can let it all go, all together.

But I don't set up to get hit. I always try to pick a spot that I think won't be found or attacked. I also move every day and never spend two nights in the same place. I pick places like halfway down a long slope, or in a narrow gully, or in a natural hollow just off the trail a ways.

I want my men to rest as much as possible at night. We hump all day. It is hard work. It is fucking-ass hard work. None of this backpacking-in-the-Sierras bullshit. Vietnam has cured my taste for camping out. I used to love walking and going to bed in the woods. But in Nam—too heavy! Waking suddenly when it's pitch dark and still, eyes darting around, ass tight. Fuck camping out, you know?

The Stream

The first thing in the morning we climb down from the ridge and into the stream. The stream forms from dozens of tiny tributaries that feed it like tiny veins quietly opening into ever larger arteries. We are on the Lang Vei side between Hill 881 South and Laos. It is real indian country, probably always will be. Thick jungle, treacherous, and steep. As we descend to the valley floor, we have to grab onto trees, branches, vines, and brush. It grows darker the farther down we go.

As we reach the floor of the small canyon, the men become quiet out of reverence. It is beautiful here. We usually talk in soft whispers in the bush, but now everyone is silent. We follow the stream as it flows a click (1,000 meters) toward Laos. The sound of soft water intermittently gurgling as it glides smoothly over the rocks that line the streambed. Ponds like terraces step the stream gently downward to the valley floor. As we descend even farther, the terraced ponds grow larger and wider until they seem to be more like shallow canals between small rapids or waterfalls that drop only a foot or two.

I see. I see my men in front of me. We are somehow like aliens in this place. The serene, quiet beauty of it all. We should not be here. Not just us, but all men. It should not be Man's place to walk here. We violate everything.

The men fall into the rhythms of the gently flowing waters. Our slow strides gliding silently through the pools of water. The stream is one, appearing not to flow at all in most parts.

A Voice

One of my lieutenants has a cassette tape player, one of the few I've ever seen. Cassette players are a new item. The lieutenant loans it to me along with a Joan Baez tape. My wife likes Joan Baez, but I would never listen to her. Like so many other brain-damaged assholes, I thought she was a pinko commie. But I listen to that tape over and over again. I should have listened to Joan earlier. What a haunting quality. "Yellow is the color of my true love's hair. . . ." Over and over I listen to it. I fall in love with Joan in Vietnam. Another warrior done in by a woman. She does it to me with the love in her voice. Men should listen to women more. About some things.

Doc My Friend

Our friendship is established the moment that we meet. There is a quietness about our respect for one another. The openness and receptivity I see in his eyes tells me that there will never be competition between us. We are more calm when we look at one another.

It is not a love based on intimacy or emotions; it is based on understanding. We are equals sharing our dignity, courage, and compassion. Like musicians in an orchestra, we play the same instruments. Men come to know each other that way without ever discussing it.

I am already a seasoned Nam vet when he arrives. He is the new regimental surgeon.

Doc likes my cocky, irreverent manner. He laughs at my callous comments about the Marines, the military, and the world in general. "Spence," he says while laughing, "is nothing sacred to you?" If I am the angry young man, then Doc is the wise old sage. Doc finished medical school and his internship before he was drafted. It's amazing to me how people like Doc My Friend are able to handle the war. I don't know what would happen to me if I had been a reluctant draftee instead of a volunteer.

Doc goes to Australia on R&R. He meets a woman in her 30s at one of those setups they have for guys on R&R in Australia. Doc barely gets this woman up to his hotel room before she lays the trip on him about how she's been married once and doesn't think she can have children. It's all her etc., etc., bullshit. Doc just wants pussy; he is not planning to go into psychiatry. Anyway, he tells her he's a doctor and shows her his uniform in the closet. Doc figures his being a doctor will get him laid—just like back home. Well, somehow before he knows it—"before I even kiss her," he says—this woman has got her pants off, and he's doing a pelvic exam on her. "Everything seems just fine!" he says.

"That's your problem, Doc." I say, "You let business and pleasure get mixed. I wouldn't dream of fighting and fucking together. Did you get any others?" I ask.

"No, I stayed with her. I would have felt guilty if I'd left."

"Jesus," I say, "I thought just us Catholics got given all that guilt shit."

"Jews taught Catholics about guilt," he answers, matter of factly.

Doc My Friend. I really like the man. He is brave. Not in a macho way like me. He is more relaxed with his manliness. I learn from him. Doc is a class guy. I always call him Doc, from the first day I meet him. He always calls me Spence. For the life of me, I cannot recall his real name.

Points

I watch some points work bush. They are just like bird dogs working. Point is the man who walks in front of everyone on patrol. I often wonder what goes on in those guy's minds as they walk point. Boy, that's a whole fucking other trip, being point. You would not want to be one of those insecure types and be a Marine point. You are always sure of one thing when it is your turn: Charlie will shoot you first. He might do a bunch of other guys, but he always does the point man first.

Marines are smart. We usually put the point man out alone. Not alone so we aren't close to him, but he's out front all alone. We give Charlie one. When a guy does point, he might act like a bird dog, but he is just bait for Charlie, is all. When we go out in the bush, we fish more than we hunt. We move to engage Charlie. We go wherever we think he is, but we rarely know. Charlie is the sneakiest cocksucker you can ever imagine. When a man does point, he knows that if he sets off an ambush, he probably won't live to get out of it himself.

Marines don't ambush like Charlie does. If we have a chance, we never shoot the first guy in line. We are always greedy. Marines pick a guy farther back for their first shot. We shoot the farthest guy out, then in, if we can.

Marines do like to unload on the motherfuckers when they have a chance. I watch the guys do six or seven NVA who are spying outside the wire at Khe Sanh. They Swiss cheese the motherfuckers. I hear only one gook round go overhead. The Marines do five or six thousand rounds. I see one machine gunner do five full belts of ammo. There are strange expressions on the faces of those Marines afterward. They look like they've been feeding on raw meat. Guys are jacked, like sharks just off a feeding frenzy. Killing is a very emotional experience.

Dead NVA

It is summer 1967, and my company is patrolling between Hill 861 and Hill 881 North. They find a dead NVA sticking up out of the mud. Besides his skeleton his clothes hold some sections of rotting flesh. He is in a bomb crater—he got done by a bomb while in his bunker. As the men gather around, the corpsman starts doing an impromptu lecture. This corpsman had been a premed student before joining the Navy. With his knowledge of Latin, he starts reciting the various names of the bones he points to with a stick. A Marine PFC from down South somewhere, a real dirty-ass, skinny ol' boy, takes about three or four Latin words. Suddenly and with great drama, he whips out his bayonet and sticks it in the skeleton's pelvic area. "And right cheers his scuzzy ol' ass," he drawls, a big toothless smile on his face. End of lecture. Marines are such cultured fuckers, aren't they?

The First Man

My first man is killed while we are on 881 South. A squad is on a night ambush just outside the wire on the Khe Sanh side of the hill. The hole in the wire is only 75 yards from my bunker, even less if I go through the bomb craters instead of along the trench line.

It is a foggy, wet, dreary-ass night. I hear it go off. Just one short burst. I know right away that something is wrong. With only one burst fired during an ambush, something is always wrong. If Charlie had walked into it, all shit would have broken loose. I think that it might have been an accidental discharge.

A man's voice coming over the radio breaks the silence. With his first words I know that something is very fucked. There is no sound like that sound in a man's voice. When a man is panicked like that and starts to talk, everyone can tell. It comes out full blast and three octaves too high.

"Squad leader's hit. Get us, get us!" he screams.

"Get out of there now!" I bark to the platoon commander over the radio.

They bring a loaded stretcher into the supply area, right next to the helicopter landing pad. When I first look at him, I know that he is dead. It is in his eyes. Wide open. Blank. It is my first time seeing a fresh-killed dead person. I'm seeing dead, smelling dead, and feeling that he's dead. This guy is fucking dead. The corpsman tells me that he's fine, that he still has a pulse. I say, "Are you sure? Are you sure?"

He has been shot high on his right shoulder. There are no exit wounds, just two small holes on the top of his shoulder. A helicopter comes out to the hill right away.

About half an hour after the helicopter departs, I get a call from battalion. He arrived a flunk. That's the term they use for someone killed in action. Like you just didn't make it in school, you know? No big deal, just a little trouble in school, and you've flunked. The fact is, he had been shot by one of his own men. He had walked into the killing zone of his own ambush.

It is pretty quiet with Charlie, so they do an investigation. A captain who commands one of my sister companies is assigned the task. He spends about 5 minutes up on Hill 881 with me. Being there under those circumstances makes him very uncomfortable. He knows that what is happening to me could just as easily happen to him. He is a lifer, a career Marine. It clearly disturbs him. Have you ever seen a guy when he's got to do something he's uncomfortable about? He kind of jerks or bounces up and down like he wants to get his balls to settle in his underwear properly and doesn't want to use his hands to move them. No hands, just bounce and jerk until the nuts settle right. While bouncing up and down he says, "Uh, I got to write you up, man."

"That's OK, I understand." We shake hands.

"I'm really sorry, man," he says just before boarding the helicopter. "I'm really sorry to have to. . . ."

So ask me if I give a fuck, I say to myself. Ask me if I give a rat's ass about a chicken-shit letter of reprimand. Five years from now the only fucker who could give a damn ain't going to be around to give anything. And that's what it's all about. The tragedy is the guy. If it makes the Marine Corps feel any better about it, I'll tattoo the motherfucking reprimand on my ass and you all can all read it any time you want. But what's that going to do for him? He is what it was all about. His death is the tragedy. Nothing else matters.

I never say a thing to any of my lieutenants about it. In our game of macho, that hit is mine to take. J.B., the colonel, was almost apologetic when he tells me that I am being reprimanded. An official letter of reprimand would be placed in my OQR. "That's fine, Colonel, I understand. It's OK, I'm getting out," I say.

Perhaps that's why they have the bulk of the fighting done by reserve officers like me. In that way the lifers can keep their OQRs clean. I wonder if people realize that fact. Many of the Marines who fight in Vietnam are draftees as enlisted men. The primary line commanders are Marine Reservists. At the company level and below, the officers like me have an *R* after the USMC. *R* for Reservist, not a fucking lifer. It was the same way in Korea and during World War II.

I never ask to see the letter of reprimand. Shit, I can guess what it says—Marines have a fucking manual for doing everything. It would say that I should have supervised the men more. Check, check, check—that's what the book says you're supposed to do. Train, train, train— every chance you get. Well, maybe that shit works when guys only spend a few weeks at a time on the line, in combat. But when you live on the line—at the edge—for over a year, the men don't want to hear any bullshit like that. If I am a private and a draftee in a fucked-up place like Vietnam and have to go out in a monsoon every day with sores all over my body and some lifer tells me to come to some chicken-shit class during my time off, in-stead of an apple for the teacher I'd bring him a short-fused grenade. Boom! One time.

I treat my men the way I want to be treated, with respect and deference. If a squad wants to be stupid, that is for the lieutenant and the squad to resolve. If a squad leader is stronger than the lieutenant, I don't take the lieutenant's side. Fuck no! I want the strongest men I can get. No man has any special shit with me because of his position or rank. I know that I am right. Every time I ask my men to move when shit is flying, they do. No one ever questions me during show time, and that's what it is all about. Trust, it's all about trust.

My first casualty was killed by one of his own men. I mourn him. I remember his face. His eyes. Blank, blue, dead eyes. The first one seems to stand out. I'll always remember. As long as I keep breathing, he'll be there. He walked into the killing zone of his own ambush. Fuck the why, he did it, is all.

The Macho of Filth

It's true what they say about the Marines at Khe Sanh. We are dirty, filthy-ass fuckers. It is the type of place that can turn anyone into a filthy scumbag real quick. Hill guys are especially dirty.

When they can, helicopters resupply our water. Water is brought in 5-gallon, gas-type cans slung under the helicopter in a cargo net. But when the weather is bad, which is most of the time, we have to get our own water. We either catch rainwater or take the long-ass hike down into the canyons below the hill. That means a couple of hours for one squad to bring back three or four cans of water. We never bathe out on the hills. Dirt is our badge of honor.

When a man walks down Main Street in Khe Sanh with red baked-in dirt on his scuzzy clothes, you know he is a hill guy. You can tell by the shade of the stain exactly what hill the guy is from. At this point there are a thousand people at Khe Sanh, but never more than a hundred guys at a time on each hill. You are considered hot shit when you are a hill guy. I wear my dirt with pride.

I fly down to Khe Sanh for meetings, and I am scuzzy as hell. When I walk down Main Street to the battalion command post unshaven and in dirty clothes, a filthy piss pot, old boots, and with no insignia of rank except an M-16 rifle, people get out of my way. It is like one of those scenes out of a western when the bad guy rides into town. Khe Sanh paperpushers scurry out of my way because hill guys are crazy. Everyone talks about us. We like our reputation. That is macho respect. We are dirty-ass, bad motherfuckers, us hill guys.

We hill guys keep our hair short. On my hill, I see to

it. I give haircuts to anyone on the hill who lets his hair get too long. I squeeze the hair clippers to make them work. It is just like doing sheep, giving haircuts that way.

One Marine is blonde and has a thick head of hair that stands straight up like the bristles on a hard brush. I am cutting his hair when I notice it: topsoil. His scalp has a fucking layer of topsoil all over. Not just dirt—that shit is ready to grow anything. His hair comes out of the topsoil just like stalks of corn. He has a layer of topsoil inside his nostrils, too. His eyes show blank, and he has a funny-ass giggle.

Up on the hills I do a 4½-month stretch without a real soap-your-ass-type shower. Dirt and grime are packed into the creases on my neck, around my shoulders, down my back, and through my midsection like the alluvial deposits of a river delta. If I stay long enough, I'll become another New Orleans.

We never use deodorant, but we do use bug juice. Lots and lots of bug juice. Insect repellent smells like kerosene. I pour slick, oily bug juice all over myself and my clothes. I don't know if it is the malaria pills or just the fact that I have been bitten too often by every species of biting insect in Vietnam, but I am very allergic to insect bites. I really douche myself with bug juice.

It all just keeps building up on me. Layer after layer, dirt and bug juice, day after day. I am turning myself into a tree. In a thousand years archaeologists will find my remains, and they will be able to tell how many days I've been out by counting my rings. I will be long-ass gone, but the bug juice and dirt won't deteriorate.

There are times I choke, gagging on myself after being out on patrol all day and sweating a fresh layer of grime on top of all the other shit. You can really imagine

M-102 105mm Howitzer

what the inside of your asshole must be like on its worst day when you smell yourself like that. That's the smell I get when I try to go to sleep after a day of patrolling out in the heat. I lie on my cot in the corner of my bunker and feel like I must have shit on myself.

We do not wear underwear in Nam. Not under our clothes, anyway. If we wear underwear, it is when we are in our bunkers. We use our skivvies for pyjamas. Skivvies should not be worn as underwear in the jungle; your balls do not like the company of skivvies. If you insist on wearing skivvies, sooner or later your balls will bloom. Fungus City, babe! And the ol' itch. If you are not careful, your whole crotch can go. Real bad crotch rot can get all the way back into your ass if you don't watch it.

We have a Mexican machine gunner. Fucker looks like an old-time bandito. Except for the different clothes, you'd swear he just stepped out of a Pancho Villa movie. This guy almost gets a nut brushing his teeth, then sucking his toothbrush dry afterward.

"Gonzales," I ask him, "do you do that after you've eaten pussy?"

"No, but he does after sucking dick," one of his squad members interjects uninvited.

"Your mowthers!" Gonzales says.

Everyone laughs.

It is a quirk of mine that I like rinsing out my mouth with warm water after brushing my teeth. I only brush my teeth in the mornings, if at all. Cold, misty mornings out on the hills. My bunker opens into a wood-lined trench where I take a can of warm water. Looking around, I see so much incredible destructive power. There are 105mm artillery pieces, machine guns, rifles, and rocket launchers all about. Ghostlike figures—the men—move about in the damp and cold. I stand there in my skivvies brushing my teeth, and I reflect on all that. All this incredible destructive power is at my command. When I look into the wet stainless-steel mirror tacked to the wall of the trench, I see my own reflection. I cannot believe that I am responsible for all this. It is so humbling standing there and feeling like the dumbest fucking bozo imaginable. Turning, I walk a few steps and push aside the canvas door to my command bunker and hear Kirby say, "Well, good morning to you, Skipper!"

CRADY

Night Action at the LZ

I appreciate helicopters. Not the pilots, necessarily, but what they fly. What takes me a day to walk, a helicopter can do in just minutes. What's more, the helicopter is my dealer. In Nam I have a real bad jones—an addiction—to food, and they bring me the shit. All kinds of good shit, like food and ammo.

You can tell which helicopter pilots are bachelors. If you have a priority medevac, a bachelor asks for smoke to mark the LZ (the landing zone). Nothing more. Fuck asking whether it is under fire or not. He expects it to be hot. You wouldn't have called his ass on a priority if it wasn't hot. Lifers or married pilots aren't that gutsy. I admire pilots who can just sit in their choppers while waiting for an emergency medevac to be loaded. He has to just sit and wait for us slow-ass grunts to load our wounded. Charlie loves to shoot up the helicopters. Boy, it must seem like forever to some of those pilots when it is like that. They have to land in the middle of a fire fight and just sit and wait for us to load. Not to be able to strike back—that's hard.

Pilots are trippers. Imagine flying out into that shit and going through a hot LZ. Twenty minutes later, you can be back at the air base drinking beer and shaking dice in the bar. That's how those helicopter pilots live. They go from a fire fight and a hot LZ to cold beer in an air-conditioned bar in half an hour or so. Tell me you wouldn't be a tripper if you did that shit for a while.

The UH-34D is the worst-riding helicopter. It is a big bubble-nosed job that has been around almost since the Korean War. Inside it always sounds like it is going to blow up because the engine is in front, and the pilots sit on top of the engine.

It is a UH-34D that crashes off Hill 861. The head corpsman calls me at around 10:00 one night to tell me that a man is delirious. The corpsman has no idea what is wrong with him. I go down to the bunker where the sick man is. His squad leader looks worried, and the sick guy looks like he is almost dead. Out cold. I call battalion and have the corpsman talk with the doctor there. Though there is intermittent fog, two UH-34Ds are sent from Khe Sanh.

We move the man to the LZ at the base of the hill. In my skivvies and a T-shirt, I wait outside my bunker for the helicopters to arrive. I'd been out on patrol in the rain that day and am airing out my feet in shower clogs.

We light our LZ with jack-off flares, which are formally referred to as Flare Hand-held Illumination. A jack-off flare looks like a silver baton about a foot and a half long. To fire it, you take the firing cap off one end, attach it to the other end, and slam it against the palm of your hand. The flare travels about 200 feet up, then—illuminated—it floats down on a parachute made of white silk with nylon cords. Nothing but the best. It burns for about one minute while falling slowly back to earth. While flickering a white, pulsating light, it hisses as it drifts downward, trailing smoke and casting fleeting, darting shadows as the parachute twists and spins. The men launch more flares, and they float toward earth, swaying back and forth like pendulums.

Both helicopters pass over the hill and turn back into the wind. One comes in to land while the other hovers nearby. I watch as the one making the landing approaches the LZ from over the steep gully. Suddenly, it just seems to lose power and drops out of sight. I can hear the pilot go to full power just before the rotor blades hit the trees. Tearing metal hitting wood. I run down the hill. "Light 'em up down there," I yell.

As a sergeant hits his flare, he slips backward. The flare goes off toward his face, nearly burning him. It shoots back up the hill and hits one of our ammo bunkers.

"You fucking cunt!" I yell at him. "Fix it!"

By now the second helicopter has turned its headlight on and is hovering over the downed chopper. One of the crewmen jumps out of the hovering helicopter. I meet the lieutenant commanding the sector that is guarding the LZ.

"Put a squad down there right away, and send down stretchers!"

Marines are scurrying around. Flares are now going off in pairs from our 60mm mortars. At any time there are from 4 to 6 flares falling, hissing, and twirling. Shadows cast over light cast over shadows. They make the dark misty night peel back its blackness. Each flare tosses its light back and forth. The helicopter hovers, waiting for its mate. The bright glare of the burning helicopter down in the gully lights the western side of the night.

A radio transmission from the rescue squad reveals that all on board got out safely. They also found the one who jumped out of the other helicopter—he's sprained both his ankles. By radio relay through battalion, we tell the airborne helicopter that its sister crew is safe. The hovering pilot comes right in with his headlights on. Doesn't say a word. Just scoots in and puts it down. Engine blades turning, engine idling, he waits. Pilots will do anything for each other.

The downed crew staggers up the hill and through the wire. It is easy to recognize them—airdales, we call them. They are bareheaded and wearing nylon jumpsuits. Shiny—especially in the light of the flares. I'm standing near the wire in my underwear, smoking a cigarette. The pilot is sweating profusely and breathing like a guy who's just done sprints.

As he walks by me, he says, "This fucking place really sucks. I'd like to get my hands on the fucker who brought me up here tonight."

"He's up on top of the hill if you want him. We call him Captain Gorilla." I'm casually pointing to the top of the steep hill above the LZ, my cigarette glowing in the light cast from the falling flares. The pilot has no fucking idea that he is talking to The Man Himself. He must think I'm the houseboy.

After the delirious man is loaded, the downed crew boards. The engine roars, the helicopter lifts up, then falls downward along the hillside off to Khe Sanh on the plateau below.

Later that night battalion radios me that the delirious

guy is drunk. Doc says the guy almost killed himself, but he'll live. One helicopter for a binge.

He returns to the hill in a few days. I leave the discipline to his lieutenant. I do not ask what is done to him. I'm sure something is. Our system of justice is personal, the way justice in such circumstances should be.

Joy Ride

Late summer, 1967. My company is going to be the first to go up into the slot above Khe Sanh since the battles of the previous spring. The Rao Quang River snakes its way through this area and alongside the northern part of Khe Sanh. You cannot see the river from Khe Sanh since the Rao Quang lies in a deep canyon.

You can tell how important the regiment feels the operation is because they order a visual flyover for me. My first and only visual reconnaissance in Nam.

The Huey flies into Khe Sanh, and I meet with the pilot and the copilot to show them on their maps the area of the slot that my company will cover. I point to certain spots that I want to fly over as low as possible.

"My orders are not to fly below 1,500 feet," the pilot deadpans to me. It is a polite fuck you, grunt.

See, helicopter pilots give grunts what they want, not what the grunt wants. I get 1,500 feet up, or I get shit. Hell, that operation tomorrow is my problem, not his. As far as he's concerned, he's doing me a favor—he's flying alone. I get only one gunship, and these guys don't like to fly by themselves. For them it's like doing point, when they have to fly alone. I'm trying to be serious with this sucker, and he's chewing gum. Like saying, "Let's go,

Huey

grunt. Let's get your dirty ass on this bird so I can get back to the bar."

I can see it from his standpoint, though. I wouldn't have taken me seriously either. A filthy, skinny fucker who wears glasses? Pilots don't wear corrective lenses. They have to have perfect vision, sight and depth. They figure only defects wear glasses. Pilots believe that only pilots are perfect. As far as airdales are concerned, infantry officers are suicidal and not completely wrapped in the brain.

Pilots always wear fancy, nylon, one-piece jumpsuits that have all sorts of zipper pockets on them. They wear shoulder holsters made from the finest cowhide. Light brown in color, just gorgeous. They carry .45-caliber pistols made of shiny gun metal with perfectly clean handle grips. Those pistols have never been fired. One look and I know. That gum chewer might know helicopters, but I know pieces. That is my trade. What really gets me are the sunglasses they wear. Joe Skier! Clean, starched-looking guys.

We finally get off the ground late that afternoon. Ignoring my request for a low flight, the pilot circles the area at high altitude.

"I can't see a fucking thing from up here!" I scream over to one of the door gunners.

He just shrugs his shoulders.

It's real loud in helicopters. All the other guys in the chopper have special flight helmets that cover the whole head. They are radioed into each other with earphones in the helmets. The gunship has rocket pods mounted on the landing skids. Two M-60 machine guns are door mounted with a gunner at each door. We do one pass and are doing the planned second pass when the chopper suddenly turns and heads toward Hill 881. The gunner yells in my ear that they've been called on a mission. Marines are being hit. Now these guys start doing their job.

Vietnam is like that. You can be in and out of the focus of the action suddenly. Everything can turn around in an instant. All of a sudden this guy is ready to come down with his chopper to treetop level. I see the smoke. WP—white phosphorus. They're marking the target. Shit, I'm thinking, I was just out here a couple of weeks ago. He does a sharp left bank and goes in, nose down. This seems so unreal to me. It is as though I'm on an amusement-park ride instead of a rocket run. I'm on the edge of my seat in the middle of the back compartment with a door gunner on each side. I'm looking between the two pilots. Noise, vibrations, rocking. Those motherfuckers do look impressive now, and they do get serious. This is their shit.

As far as gunship pilots are concerned, grunts are just bird dogs who are meant to flush game for them to shoot.

That's all we are. Except lots of times we're flushing shit for these guys, and they aren't available. Dogs always have to be there, gunship pilots don't. For a grunt it is as though everyone else just seems to enter your life and depart—suddenly.

There is a horrendous explosion. I think we've taken a hit, but it was the rockets firing. I see them—weaving, darting, lines of smoke. Trails of smoke converging in front of me like little birds with smoke coming out of their asses. The gunner had let all 16 rockets go at the same time. The noise of them going off was the loudest bang I've ever heard. There are no doors on these helicopters, and the rockets are right outside.

The gunners point their machine guns straight forward in fixed positions and start firing. The gunners pull the triggers, but the pilot does the aiming. We are maybe 75 feet off the ground.

I see the Marines. We come in on the strafing run right over them. Marines lie scattered about on the ground in the prone position, facing where the rockets had just hit some 80 yards in front of them. I notice one Marine. He is rolled on his left side and is looking up as we come right over him. He has a shit-eating grin on his face like a kid at a party who's watching the guys with the keg of beer arrive. That kind of smile.

Black Dudes and Other Bad Asses

You know what Vietnam clears up once and for all? All the bullshit that's been told about the black guy not having it. The white man has long since stopped kidding himself about whether the black man could kick his ass in a fistfight. Even so, before Vietnam you'd hear shit about black guys not having it when the chips were down in battle. Any motherfucker that tells you he's a Vietnam vet and a Marine and that black guys don't fight well is a liar. I see the brothers kick ass lots of times. Black dudes maintain their dignity throughout. They can still walk, be, and unload. Charlie does not intimidate the brothers. I want my men to be that way. Unintimidated by anything.

Sure, some of them were hoods or criminals back home. What do you expect, John Wayne? Kiss my ass. Line Marines aren't John Wayne types. When they're killers, they aren't. All different races of Marines kill well where I am.

I don't give a fuck what he did back in the world. What he did in the world is the world's problem. He is in Nam with me, and I like him the way he is. I like a guy who just can't wait to get off on somebody. My guys aren't jumpy, either. I don't have many accidental discharges; when they shoot, it is deliberate.

One guy in Delta Company is one of the most obvious hoodlums imaginable. Rodriguez, a big dude from Detroit. He has a Spanish surname, but that man is all black. He had participated in the riots in Detroit and brags about all the looting and burning that he'd done. That is his badge of macho. Some of his teeth are missing. He is strutting his stuff outside one day.

"Hey, Rodriguez!" I call to him. "What the fuck is that you're wearing?"

His flak jacket is open. He is shirtless and has on several necklaces of love beads, which I have never seen before.

"It's part of my culture," he says matter of factly.

"Yeah, well put your culture where I can't see it."

"Why should I, Skipper?"

"Because my fucking culture says so. And zip up your flak jacket."

I like him, but I never let on that I do. I feel so very comfortable with his kind of people. I guarantee you, guys like Rodriguez are my best fighters—guys like him and the guys who came out of the stockades as deserters.

You think about it. Any guy who says fuck it and leaves has got some balls. Balls are what it takes to unload on someone, especially if the other guy is unloading back on your ass. Yep, if my company walked down the worst streets in New York, I guarantee that even the toughest motherfuckers would get their asses back inside the buildings. We are that bad.

Now some of these guys are just going from fix to fix or bottle to bottle. They did their time like that, as bad-ass Marines. Now they're just doing themselves, day after day. Being a bad ass can give you some, not just let you get.

None of us think about that in Nam. We do not think about what is going to happen when we are back in the world. That is the least of our worries. I can just see some dork career counselor coming out to the field and telling me, "Well, Ernest, it's time you started thinking about what you're going to do with the rest of your life." That wet-dream would take one incoming barrage and change his tune to "We have just got to get out of this hostile motherfucker right-ass now!"

Being a bad ass is the best way to stay alive in the field. You have to want to kick ass or you are dead. Marines hate defense. They want to do somebody.

Killer

He has that look—that special look—and he has a reputation. It is either his second or third tour when he joins Delta Company in the late fall of 1967. All his time had been on the line. That he is just a corporal E-4 indicates the problems he must have had back in the world. An alcoholic, Southern Comfort is his favorite drink. His platoon commander is intimidated by him and leaves him completely alone. Without question he is the best man we have in the company. The best killer, that is.

The line time has made him look like he is in his late 30s or early 40s. More than anything, his eyes stand out. The same type of eyes that you see in prisons or in mental institutions. A man lives through his eyes.

Killer is as close to death as you can be. His entire self is only this: He can no longer exist outside Vietnam. So well adapted to killing has he become that now he cannot leave. Society has made him a killer. Society sent him to the edge, where he has spent so much time that he can no longer function to acceptable standards in the world. He is an addict. War is his jones.

He is almost godlike to us. Though his leader, I also worship him. He gives the ultimate love that we know: You can always count on Killer being there when shit hits. That is when he becomes a great soloist. He comes alive like the phoenix; he rises and does his thing.

Killer is in his early 20s.

Violence

What is violence? To me it is a strong, sensual perception. So strong is it that all senses are affected. It is one of those things that must be experienced to be understood. Violence is about feelings—very powerful, heady feelings. It takes macho to stay in such a game. Macho is the costume worn in a game of violence. How do you wear yourself? People who play with violence for any length of time get burned out for anything else. It's just too much feeling; their senses get shorted out.

Holding Macho

Booze helps me hold my macho. Younger guys tend to use drugs. I understand that the Marines are on a strict program that discourages alcohol and drug use. Urine tests. What bullshit! A man has to have something to fuel or hold the macho. He needs something to keep the lid on. You can't expect to just turn a killer on and off like a fucking appliance. He's not going to be able to chew ass one minute and sit quietly like an unplugged Cuisinart the next.

Bad Boys

We come in off a long-range patrol and enter Khe Sanh combat base up by the abandoned coffee plantation. As soon as we clear the wire, my guys break up into small groups and head for our company area. None of this marching-in-formation bullshit like they do back in the world. We are field dirty and worn.

106

Main Street, Khe Sanh, is a rutted dirt road 15 to 20 feet wide. Along the south side of the airstrip, the street runs the length of the base. Main Street looks like everything that you would imagine a lawless town to look like. Green tents, bunkers with sandbagged walls, tin-roofed, open-sided buildings on stilts. On Main Street you see flyboys, Seabees, and sundry characters. You can always spot the Seabees, who work on the airfield—they are the fat ones. Navy eats in their sleep, I swear. Artillery turds walk with a drug-addict bounce. It must come from standing too close to the cannons firing.

The poges are also easy to spot. They wear clean jungle utilities and look like they have just taken a shower. A poge is a guy who isn't directly involved in killing—a Marine clerk, for example. You pronounce the word like *poke* except with a hard g. Poges from the base stand silently, almost reverently, watching us pass. The dirt is slick from a mist so thick that it is almost a light rain. There's a slight skidding and a crunch under our boots. The poges are afraid to look us in the eyes for very long. Hill guys look right through people. Right into and through them. Line guys sit apart from everyone and everything else. We are different is all. We are the crazies among the crazy.

Being Crazy

It is perfectly acceptable amongst us line guys for any one of us to be out-of-his-fucking-mind crazy. Our world is insanity. Even the dumbest ones amongst us know that. Being strange is not looked upon as any sort of aberration, it is just seen as a part of one's personality—like a sense of humor. Being strange, weird, or a drooling lunatic is no problem at all, as long as you do your job. If you do your job, who you are is your business. There is a very strict unwritten code of ethics, but being strange is not only acceptable, it is viewed with great relish.

Strange is our way of dealing with it. It is the kind of place that you need an extra dimension to deal with the tension of being so up all the time. Being strange fills a need. Strange can find humor for yourself and others. You need to laugh. You would die if you had no chance to laugh.

Strange is a simple humor. Macho humor. I can't think of any guy who goes through Khe Sanh who doesn't get strange. As long as you do what you are supposed to do for your company, then you can be any weirdo that you want. I never take a guy out of the field for just being strange. Shit, no. I just figure he is well adjusted to the place. I know what the fuck I am doing. I also know that I am strange.

Crazy Doc

Our battalion surgeon, Crazy Doc, is strange. Semi-borderline crazy motherfucker, and brave. His thing is doing jungle sores.

Jungle sores can be anything from the size of a tiny puss-topped zit to an inflammation that eats right down to your shinbone. Jungle sores usually grow on your hands, arms, or legs. We get jungle sores because of the filth. A simple cut or scratch can easily become a jungle sore. I am an antiseptic-using motherfucker.

Crazy Doc occasionally visits us out on the hills.

Whenever he sees a guy with sores, he starts acting like a Latino when he gets near pussy. Doc really gets into cleaning and popping them. For the ones that are small, he uses a syringe with the needle removed. He laughs his ass off while trying to see how quickly he can fill the syringe. I remember one day in particular. While Crazy Doc does the guy in the supply tent, I sit eating cookies and drinking chocolate. One guy writhing in pain while two others are laughing their asses off.

Crazy Doc is a rare breed for an MD. Saying on him is that he'd give anything to be a rifleman. He's that far out. Crazy Doc is all the way out. He extended in Vietnam and did two tours in a row. He loves the bush.

A Touch

He is a sergeant who transferred to my company in the late fall of 1967. He had been in the battles around Con Thien, the worst pounding the Marines have taken so far. He displays classic shell-shock symptoms. Like a dog that can't stop shaking or moving, he is always nervous. We are preparing to leave on a long-range patrol in an area south of the base. It has not been patrolled for a long time. As I watch the men form in small units preparing to depart, he approaches me.

"Sir, may I speak with you a moment?" he asks quietly.

His eyes dart from side to side, as mine bore straight in on him. By now I have learned to decipher such lead ins.

"I'm going to get out. Twelve fucking years in the Corps, and I'm getting out," he says. "I don't want to do it anymore. I'll do anything you want, but please don't make

CH-53

me go out there. I've had enough." His head and body jerk in uncontrolled sudden movements.

"Yeah, Sarge," I say, "that's fucking great, but your tour ain't over yet, and you're not bleeding. So get your fucking mortar section and your ass ready to go because you're going. Get the fuck out of the Marine Corps on your time. This is my time now, and you're with me, sweetheart."

What a spooky place our objective is—I can understand why no one patrols it. As we are moving up a stream, the point reports seeing smoke up ahead. I send the word forward to shoot anything that moves. We are moving in column in the stream—terrain is too thick to navigate. As I move forward, I see the sergeant quietly deploying his 60mm mortar section on a small sand bar in midstream. My legs quietly slide forward against the current of the stream. Pressing my knees and thighs, the water reluctantly gives around me. I move by him, passing on his right. He is crouched next to the mortar tube. In front of him fresh green mortar rounds lay spread like a good day's catch of trout. As I pass, I touch him on his shoulder with my left hand. Not a pat; a respectful placement of my hand upon his shoulder. He glances up as I move forward. We say nothing.

We find only the remains of a fire. Charlie ran that day, but the sergeant did not. I don't know if he got out of the Marines or not, but he got his dignity back.

R&R

Late fall, 1967. I guess the field is starting to get to me. J.B., the battalion commander, calls and tells me to go down to Da Nang for two days of R&R. I have been doing hill duty or patrols continuously since my arrival in Nam. J.B. probably noticed that my feet weren't hitting the ground when I walked. I must be wired. You know, jacked up—not jumpy—just jacked up. Line time does that to you.

I have a couple ex classmates from Officers' Basic School stationed down at Da Nang. They are both pilots now. I look them up and go to stay with them.

I go straight out of the bush wearing my dirty field clothes—no bath. I get a direct flight from Khe Sanh to Da Nang in a CH-53 helicopter. A dead helicopter gunner is onboard the same flight. His last ride out. He got nailed up in the slot right over and up a ways from where I had just been on patrol. The gunner had been on a recon insert (a reconnaissance mission), and Charlie had been right there. Recon was always getting the shit kicked out of them.

This dead Marine is in a black body bag. Tag is on the zipper, just like a fucking piece of luggage. L.CPL So-and-so, unit so-and-so. Some poge who is on the flight inadvertently steps on the bag as he tries to cross to the other side of the helicopter. A Marine colonel also on board goes completely bullshit. "Get the fuck away from that Marine!" he screams at the poge. For the rest of the flight, that poor poge looks like a dog that's been whipped.

My pilot friends live in a typical Da Nang hootch. It is a tin-roofed rectangular one-room building with ply-wood floors and screened-in sides. All the buildings are up off the ground as a precaution against flooding. They have cots, wall lockers, and a refrigerator. Ice-cold beer, I go right for the cold beer. They're both looking at me and saying, "Hey, man, we got some new clothes and great showers here. Would you like to wash up?"

"Fuck the wash, girls," I say, burping the residue of a fresh-killed can of Miller's. "If you guys don't mind, I'm going to get very fucking polluted. I been out so fucking long, I don't know how fucking filthy I am." I tell them I want to go to the big Navy officers' club. I've heard that they do grilled steaks there with sit-down service and a real live stateside bar. Bear in mind that I've been doing mostly C rations for over 5 months. I am half shit-faced drunk in no time.

I don't know how I talk them into it, but I get them to take me to the officers' club without even changing my dirty clothes. They have a taxi service for officers in Da Nang. Believe it? The taxis are pick-up trucks with wooden benches in back. The entire truck bed is cabbed over. Gray. They are painted Navy fucking gray. Each taxi has a radio and an enlisted squid driver. They have a regular phone system in Da Nang. You can just call up and get a cab. Free. Riding in that cab—it gets to me. Where I just was, and then this. I'm in a war, then I'm in a cab. This morning I'm checking out a war scene, and this afternoon I'm in a fucking cab pissed to the gills and going to dinner. I couldn't handle this all the time, I think to myself. I'd lose my concentration if I had to keep jumping back and forth like this.

We get to the Navy club early. The air conditioning hits me going through the door. It chills me. I am aware now of how filthy I am. It is as though the air conditioning is freezing all the grime on me, and I can feel it all crusting up. My odor, which I was not aware of until then, emerges. We are seated at tables with tablecloths. Real plates. Glasses, silverware. My two friends are captains and are properly dressed in clean jungle utilities. We get very strange looks.

Two Navy lieutenants dressed in whites are seated at a table next to us. It is obviously distressing to those two fuckheads to have to eat next to someone dressed the way I am. It probably isn't just my dress, it is my whole drunken manner.

I establish good eye contact with them, pick up my steak in my right hand, and start chewing it. After I put it down, I wipe my hand on my shirt, take a swig of beer, and do a loud burp. "Delicious!" I say, smacking my lips.

I am drunk. Completely. I get into a fight at the Air Force place where we go next, the Gunslinger Officers' Club.

The next morning I awake still clothed and on one of the cots at my friends' hootch. Besides the banging in my head, I feel a dull throbbing pain in the knuckles in my hands. Quickly I feel my face for any lumps. My face feels fine.

"How'd I do?" I say to my airdale friend as I stagger outside. He is seated on the front steps having a cup of coffee.

"Oh, you did real good, Ernie. You managed to fuck up my chances of ever going back to that place for a while. Just what is your problem with the Air Force, anyway? You started it, you know."

"Did we get busted by the MPs?" I ask sheepishly.

"No, we got you out of there before it got real bad." He is not angry with me. Almost a compassionate look is on his face, and he smiles. "You fucking grunts are all nuts. I guess you wouldn't be grunts if you weren't." There is a resignation in his tone, a recognition of a tragic reality.

When I get back, J.B. asks me if I had a good time. I tell him that I must have because I can't remember. That's how fighters have been clearing their pipes for centuries. A ritual alcoholic bath, then reprimed and ready. I never get drunk on the line. I have too much respect for the field. But I did douche myself real good in Da Nang that time.

THE CHANGE

December 1967. It all begins to come together. The reality and the change. My awakening. The realization of my disillusionment.

We are to do a battalion-sized helicopter landing north of Khe Sanh up in the slot. It is as far out as they let anyone go. I had patrolled the area a couple of times with just my company and had not been hit. The area where we are to land is thick with elephant grass. While waiting on the airstrip at Khe Sanh, we receive word that the landing zone is hot. For the first time it feels like I am finally going in the way I want to. If it's hot, I'll be right on the motherfuckers. No crawling-around-out-in-the-jungle bullshit. Right now. One time. I want it that way.

What a surprise I get. The landing zone is hot because the elephant grass has caught on fire from our own artillery prep. The first wave goes in when the fires are just starting. The second wave, which I am with, gets caught in a backburn. As I run down the stern ramp of the CH-46 helicopter, all I can see is a wall of flame coming right for me. People are running in every direction, trying

CH-46

to get away from the flames that are raging. We make a run for a gully that has a stream at the base. Smoke, haze, and yelling fill the afternoon air. What a fucking fire drill. We almost die in that shit. After half an hour it is over. My company is scattered and has to be reassembled.

That was the first time that my own artillery almost caused my death. I should have associated better. All my focus had been on the enemy, but it was my own that almost did me. I feel fucked.

I remember an artillery officer who gave a lecture when I was in Officers' Basic School. He said, "Yes, gentlemen" (we were all so civilized then), "infantry is the queen of battle, but we in artillery like to think that we're the king because we put the balls just where the queen wants them." Well, arty—artillery—must have thought that I was Greek. The only place artillery puts anything that I notice is in my ass.

116

On this sweep I am feeling contact all the time, even though the landing was a false alarm. The four rifle companies are sweeping independently in a westerly direction toward the river. We go one, two days—nothing but a lot of signs. Tracks made by NVA shoes are on most of the trails. On the third day Alpha Company, which is north of my company, hits right next to the trail—the very same trail that I am now crossing farther south. Sounds of gunfire echo down the valley. They'll flush them toward me.

I set up my men around a small opening that the trail runs through. It is a small meadow with tall grass but no trees. Probably it had been a ville. Thick jungle growth rings the small clearing. I conceal two machine guns at the base of this meadow—the best fields of fire are from that point. The rest of the battalion is to the north and east of me; to the west and nearby is the river, which runs north and south. I scurry about like a housewife getting ready for a party, a surprise party for Charlie. I assign the fields of fire for the men, just like a housewife telling everyone where to stand and where to throw the confetti when the guests arrive.

I settle on the left side of our ambush site on a slight mound. I can see the trail and all of the meadow clearly from my position. Everyone is well concealed. It is quiet.

I'll never have another opportunity like this. I feel—for once—that if Charlie comes, it is going to be all my party. Thumping sounds of my heartbeat pulsate in my ears. As I lie there, each breath taken is precious and savored. The leaves and rot upon which I lie hidden moisten my thighs and elbows. The dampness of the jungle seeps into me. As one with the earth, we lie in wait. Still as the forest but deadly plants are we.

117

I am thinking, what the fuck are you gonna do, Charlie, caught with your pants down the way we always are? You gonna punch back or boogie the fuck out? I know that he'll split. I know he won't throw with us. If he steps out into that clearing, as soon as we open up, he'll bug out toward the river. Charlie already knows we are above and to the east of him. The only one he doesn't know about is me. I maneuvered my company all day, quietly, through the low ground and deep in the bush. We now not only cover the trail, but I had placed a blocking force between the clearing and the river. If Charlie steps into that clearing, we will burn his ass.

Listening on the battalion radio, I hear that Alpha Company has hit a bivouac area. They caught Charlie at home. My heart is banging away in my ears, sweat pours off my face. It is all that I can do to keep myself from hyperventilating. Images flash through my mind as I lie there and think, holy Christ, Charlie is flushed and is coming right toward me. We can take these motherfuckers out.

We stay in the ambush for less than an hour. Battalion becomes impatient and orders me to move out and across the Rao Quan River. They are worried about making our objective before nightfall, an objective that had been set that morning before we hit Charlie. I am supposed to occupy an abandoned ville on the other side of the river. I argue. I tell them that I have an ideal ambush site established. We can easily stay all night. I keep telling them what an excellent spot we are in. We know where we are and already have good fields of fire laid out. We can burn 'em. There are less than a couple of hours of daylight left.

The assistant operations officer, the S-3, is a real

prick. Lifer fucker. Spent his first 6 months in Okinawa and will only do 6 months in Vietnam. He wants his plan done his way. A real flexible cocksucker.

It really pisses me off to have to pull out of that ambush site. I am seething as we leave.

I never believe in rushing my men to any objective, but now we are chasing the dying daylight. I goad my lead platoon to keep moving. The prick from battalion keeps pimping me about how slowly we are going. We find a place to ford the river. Round, smooth stones line the bottom 2 to 4 feet beneath the surface of the swift-flowing waters. The far bank, lined with trees, lies some 100 feet away. Swift currents of water bend around my legs and push at me as I cross.

As I climb the far bank and turn to watch the others crossing, I notice one of the men bent forward with his face down in the water. He looks like someone bobbing for apples at Halloween. He is our new artillery forward observer, just out of artillery school and new incountry. This is the same cocksucker who has been checking my map constantly during the operation to confirm our position. He and his glasses remind me of a Jerry Lewis character. Halfway across the river, he had dropped his glasses. He looks like a dog trying to bite something underwater. I cannot believe this guy. That jerk-off finds 'em. He comes up out of the water with this big shit-eating grin on his face just like he's just won some circle-jerk contest. We've been chasing Charlie all day, and this motherfucker is getting off on his own fucking glasses? I call the other artillery spotter over. I've known this NCO since I've been with the company. "Get that motherfucker away from me," I say. "I don't give a fuck what you do, but you keep that shithead away from me. I don't want that cocksucker calling any fire missions for me, understand?" I don't know what they do with him, but I never see him again after that operation.

By now, I've come to trust my opinions of others. I don't agonize about my decisions. This is not a game where guys are playing for high-school letters. I think I save some of the officers I bench, but I am not really concerned about them. I figure any man who makes it out alive doesn't have a thing to say. It's the ones who want to stay alive, who need to stay alive, but don't that count. I begin to see that. I begin to see myself differently.

To that point I had just visualized events, and the way I visualized them was the way they unfurled. I had been Lord God Almighty while waiting to burn Charlie. If I could have stayed there, my way, I'm sure Charlie would have come to my party. Every one that I could have put in my sights, I would have shot. I would have killed every single one of them.

But the assistant operations officer hadn't listened to God. He pulled us out of the ambush site and put our asses way out in the open. Who was he to get us killed as a result of his ineptitude? He had us on the end of a string, and he wasn't just jerking the men around, he was jerking me around too. No longer am I the detached unfeeling eye that sees all the options. I have no options. I am in the same shit with everyone else. I am vitally involved. I am right there.

Having to leave that ambush site is like hearing the bell ring just when you feel like you can knock the other guy out. I feel tense and am still pissed—a bad feeling flows through me going into that old ville. The ville site is rapidly returning to jungle. There are fresh NVA tracks everywhere. We start to set up for the night. Darkness edges across the sky. I drop my pack. In the center of the ville where the paths intersect, a tree has fallen. It is 3 feet thick and smooth, the bark has fallen away. With my hand I feel the grain of the weathered wood, cracking now that the skin is gone. This will be my command post for the night. My radio operators squat near and around me. They drop their gear. No words are spoken, my intentions are intuitively known. My rifle rests on the log. The forward edge of the company perimeter is 60 to 70 feet off to my right side, my gun side. I begin scanning the area around me, selecting my fields of fire should an attack come. Thick brush is all around me, not solid thick, but thick enough so you have to zigzag to get around it. Charlie won't be able to rush me, I am thinking.

I see a twig flying like it's just been cut. The first shot goes by my right ear with a loud crack. My helmet is off and lying on the ground. I think I'm hit. My first move is a half dip, then a semisquat, then I go all the way down. Two more shots go right over me. A couple more hit to my left side. There's screaming, then the sounds of thrashing and crashing. Sounds in the bushes like a dogfight. I jump over the log. My rifle is now in my right hand. "Let's go!" I yell.

I run zigzag, zigzagging around the brush. One of my men has taken cover on the ground 8 feet away, lying perpendicular to me. He's reacting to hearing me coming through. He whirls toward me with his rifle. His eyes are lit up and bulging out. His rifle comes right for my chest. He's focused right on my chest, just like a Marine is supposed to. He is going to take me out. I realize that I'm not wearing my helmet—he thinks I'm a gook. "Hey, fuck, it's me!" I scream.

His eyes jerk up to mine. My eyes freeze him. Then

he shakes like a dog shitting razor blades when he realizes that he's almost taken out the Old Man.

Two of the men had been beating down fields of fire in front of their position. The thick grass around them lies trampled. One man is lying quietly on his side, wounded. Men are running all around us now. Another man flat on his back, arms outstretched like he is on the cross. In one hand he holds an AK-47 NVA rifle. Crimson wet across the lower part of his shirt shows that he's been gut shot.

"Look what's happened to me, Skipper," he cries out. He's pleading with me to help him, to fix him. He's looking at me and gasping between cries.

"I'm getting you out son," I say. "I swear to God I'll fucking get you out. Priority medevac!"

The radio operator puts in the call, then returns to me. "They're asking for you, Skip," he says.

"Fuck 'em, I'm busy." The platoon sergeant asks if we should recon by fire. The jungle is too thick; it would be useless. "Fuck no," I say.

My man is gut shot through the back. The exit wound is near his navel. The bayonet of the AK-47 rifle that he holds is snapped open. Charlie was going to stick him. Corpsmen are working silently. Bandages and red sticky blood are everywhere. Paper scattered about from the torn bandage wrappings. Jerking, broken visions. I run back and forth checking, searching for the best possible LZ for the medevac. Battalion is giving my radio operator holy hell because I won't talk to them on the radio. He just keeps sweet-talking the shit out of them. He doesn't bother me while I'm busy. I'm not ready to talk.

Blades of the helicopter twang as they hit the limb of a nearby tree. A hurricane roars around us as we load the two wounded men aboard. Roaring winds swirl and slap at us, abating as the chopper rises slowly. Suddenly, all is still around us again. Only the popping of the helicopter is a distant reminder of what just happened. No longer can I see the ground I stand upon. Darkness has suddenly descended.

I finally talk to J.B., the colonel. I am emotionally drained. He senses my feelings. Speaking in a slow, hushed manner, I tell him what happened. We got hit. They just stumbled into us, maybe they were part of the unit that Alpha Company hit earlier. I don't know for sure.

The clear hiss of the open mike breaks the silence. After a long pause J.B. says, "Good luck tonight. This is Blackbud 6, out."

Right after J.B. gets off, the assistant S-3 comes on over the radio. "Did you return fire Blackbud Delta?"

"Negative."

"Roger and out." Like tsk, tsk.

Two of my guys get dumped on because that motherfucker wants his plan followed, and now he's implying something. That lifer motherfucker doesn't know the situation. People far removed from the reality always seem to possess such certainty, such righteousness.

I learn what had happened to the two wounded men. After shooting them one of the gooks tried to bayonet the kid that was gut shot. He took the gook's rifle away during the scuffle. That's my kind of man. Charlie got some on him, but he got some too. You didn't kill him, Charlie, I checked. He lived, and he got your fucking rifle.

That night my executive officer gives me a can of smoked oysters. Realizing what a trying day it has been, he seeks to ease my depression. "Here, Skip, you'll love these," he says. I'm hungry. I eat the oysters and all the food I have in my pack. Fuck breakfast, we'll be resupplied tomorrow.

Dark, quiet, no moon. The only sounds are of me puking. All the shit I have in me comes up. "Goddamn, that was delicious," I say, trying to act cool. Nobody says a thing to me that night or later. My radio operators know. They know I am letting off steam. They are probably happy that I am letting it off that way and not taking it out on them.

The operation is terminated early. We are called back to Khe Sanh the next day. It is a one-day march back. A cakewalk. What a difference a day makes.

THE SIEGE: SURROUNDED

Guys who did Khe Sanh measure their time differently than most guys who did Nam. Nam vets measure their lives before and after Nam, but guys who did Khe Sanh measure Nam with subclassifications: pre-siege and post-siege.

The Chain of Command

Fall 1967. Something is going on with Charlie again.

We are moving, company in column. I am moving with the forward platoon. Point is just crossing a stream at the base of the ridgeline, an unmanned ridgeline that has a view of Khe Sanh base. I'm halfway through a dry rice field that slants toward the stream. The field has been cut and is just stubble. A hill of dense brush is beyond.

A loud clacker goes off—like one of those wooden jobs you'd use at a New Year's party. Charlie uses clackers to communicate in the field. Goddamn! I think I am going to get it. I think it is the signal to set off an ambush. The sound comes from halfway up the hillside. The men in the

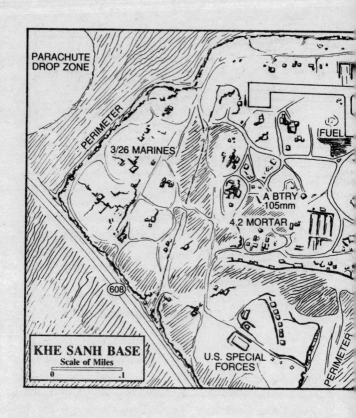

PARACHUTE
DROP ZONE

PERIMETER

3/26 MARINES

FUEL

A BTRY
105mm

4.2 MORTAR

(608)

KHE SANH BASE
Scale of Miles
0   .1

U.S. SPECIAL
FORCES

PERIMETER

open are all down on one knee, pointing their rifles up
along the hill in front. I tell arty to set up a possible
mission.

Charlie runs that morning. He doesn't want to go at it
with me. Good thing, too—my ass is all the way in the open.

One of my men finds a map. One of the NVA had
been sketching the base. I report to battalion that we have

scattered a possible NVA recon unit. I report the map find.

We continue our patrol throughout the day. It starts raining soon after we get on the ridgeline. We don't have more than an hour and a half of daylight left. We are getting ready to set in for the night when I get a radio message.

Return to base immediately, I am told. I go at it on the radio with the assistant S-3. I tell him there is no way I can get back to base before dark. I would have to go right back over the spot where we found signs of Charlie. It would be dark. It's been raining all day. The stream is going to be raging. I tell him I'm not coming in. I am fuming. I tell him he can have me relieved tomorrow, but I won't endanger my men tonight.

J.B. gets on the radio. Very calm. Tells me he understands. He fully appreciates my concern. He says he needs it. It is regiment. That important, he says. He tells me he'll explain when I get in. He doesn't have to say any more. I will not embarrass him with the regimental CO.

I call my platoon commanders together. They are pissed. We decide to go in column, running one guy behind the other. We know that if we are hit, we'll get our clocks cleaned.

We move in a fast walk, slow jog with all our gear. We slip and slide on the ridgeline. When darkness hits we close up the column. Guys start goosing each other. It's so ridiculous by now that the men are laughing and joking. I stop the column twice to tell them to shut the fuck up. It doesn't work. They are like a bunch of girls at a slumber party. We could be ambushed and annihilated—I have made them risk themselves to that degree. They might have to obey me, but they aren't going to give me the last bit of defiance they need as men—the defiance of laughter. What am I going to do, send them to Vietnam?

The stream is a torrent when we reach it about 8:00. The first guy who tries to cross is knocked down, loses all his gear, and almost drowns. I have big guys, good swimmers, strip down. I join them, and we link arms and form a human chain across the stream. The stream is less than knee high that morning; now it's waist to chest high and raging. It is a nightmare come true. I stand there realizing that I had almost got burned by Charlie that morning, and tonight I'm doing it to myself. All at the very same spot.

All the men cross on the upstream side. Each one looks me in the eye as he comes by me in the chain. Some show terror, others are pissed and look it. There isn't a thing I can say. Every one who wants to give me a fuck-you stare, I let 'em. I am wrong. I have betrayed their trust.

We all get in safely about 9:30. I go to see the colonel. I am so pissed, I want to hit something. I stop and kick the shit out of the walls—anything—along the way. I am so jacked up. I'm moving like a guy who's got to piss real bad—a man who has got to keep moving, jumping, or he'll piss himself. I kick the ground to keep from going out of control.

I'm still fuming when I reach J.B.'s bunker. He tries to disarm me right away. He's got staff present, and he has a big shit-eating grin on when he sees me. Jumps up, eyes sparkling, grabs my hand, and starts pumping it. Slapping me on the back he says, "Congratulations, Delta 6." When J.B. is being formal, he calls you by your battalion call sign. "Some of the guys at regiment said you'd never make it in. You did just great, just great. Great patrolling," he says.

I say, "Colonel, can I talk to you alone?" I know my eyes are lit up, and I can barely stay still. I'm all jerky and twitching from anger. We go to an empty area. He lets me talk—lets me get fucking pissed off. He just watches me very sympathetically. If one of my lieutenants gave me that kind of shit, I'd have punched him in his mouth. But J.B.

is a class guy. J.B. knows I did it for him. I risked myself and all my men for him.

I tell him I want an explanation. I remind J.B. that my credibility with my men has been severely strained. I want to know exactly why that fucker at regiment made J.B. order us in.

"Ernie, I tried to tell him. I argued as much as I could. That's why you got the word so late."

A couple of months earlier, Charlie Company had been on the same ridgeline. The CO of the company was relieved of command for refusing to move down across the open fields that I had just crossed. The commander of Charlie Company was right: He would have exposed his men completely if he had followed orders. He was much more principled than I was.

J.B. appreciates that he did not have to relieve another of his line officers of command. He tells me that the regimental commander is a man of "feelings"—he has strong premonitions. He felt we were going to be attacked at the base with my company out. Two companies were on 861 and 881 South. Regiment felt that the base was too vulnerable.

"What?" I say. "We got a fucking swami with a crystal ball for a regimental CO? He's got enough poges on this base to make up another company."

"Not a rifle company, Ernie."

No one attacks that night. Regimental CO never even says thank you. I risk my whole company for that cocksucker's wet dreams, and he doesn't even say thank you.

Only luck saved me that day. I used up a whole bunch of luck stupidly, but J.B. is the type of guy who can get you to do that.

I do get even, though. I start a rumor about the

regimental CO being a cuckoo nut. Yep, I tell my radio operators and lieutenants, who I know tell their squad leaders. Once it hits that level, it goes Marine Corps-wide.

Moving into Town

My company is assigned as the reaction force at the base at Khe Sanh. We will support any sector that needs reinforcement during an attack. We move onto the base, where we are centrally located near graves registration and the hospital and just up from the garbage dump. As more reinforcements arrive, most are placed at the northern part of the base. One battalion of ARVN Rangers is placed at the southern end of the runway on the Lang Vei side. My company is just right of center for a bull's-eye shot from the rockets on 881 North. That's where most of the rockets come from. For Charlie's artillery from Co Roc in Laos, we are just left and down from the bull's-eye. Regiment, supplies, the Seabees, medical, fuel—almost everyone is cramped on one side of the airfield in a confined area. Khe Sanh quickly takes on the appearance of a shantytown.

Home on R&R

As January 1968 draws to a close, I put the shantytown behind me. For R&R I go home to Hawaii. R&R is weird for me. I can't come down. My family acts as though nothing is wrong, but I am up. On the outside quiet and cool, but up on the inside. I've spent 6 months getting to where I can handle emotions well. I'm not going to let my guard down by feeling things.

The last thing that I want to think about on R&R is where I have just come from, but the first night home I see myself on the "CBS Evening News," walking Hill 881. The segment had been filmed weeks earlier. Robert Schakne is the reporter, a tiny man in a piss pot who looks like something out of World War II. I remember how psyched Schakne had been and how my guys had snickered and hooted, "Wow, Skipper, you're fucking Hollywood!"

What comes out on the national news is a cut on bunkers. I am showing him an old NVA bunker on 881 when he asks me who has better bunkers, Marines or NVA. I tell him Marines. What did he expect me to say: "Oh, without question it's the gooks 'cause we're all stupid."

Reporters are always questioning and doing comparisons. Marines would go crazy if they had to question everything like that. Reporters always have an advantage over us: They can walk away from the shit; we can't. I wonder if reporters ever understand that. Shooting film and shooting are two different things.

Bingo

Khe Sanh is hit on my last day of R&R. I feel like a chicken shit for not being there with my company. That's how I return—pissed at myself for not being there.

A CH-46 helicopter takes me back to the base. No trouble getting connections to Khe Sanh now. All hell has broken loose. Khe Sanh is now the hottest show in Nam. Tents are still up, I notice during the approach, but everything has changed since I left. There is an ominousness, a harshness everywhere. Next to the landing pad, full fuel bladders lie scattered like large pillows. Almost like a Charlie Chaplin movie, people are moving in a quick, jerky fashion—even the black dudes. Incoming rockets and artillery had changed things.

We take incoming within 15 minutes of when I land. I come in wearing a soft cap, and it feels good to put my piss pot on again. I'd missed my piss pot while I was on R&R. That thing fit me real comfortable; it rode me just right. After wearing one for a while, you rock your head differently when you walk. I also put on my flak jacket, which I never wore before. Flak jacket would not stop a rifle shot, just shrapnel. But life is about adjusting. Khe Sanh meant rockets and artillery, and rockets and artillery are all about shrapnel. Everyone looks fat in a flak jacket. They have square nylon plates sewn in individual packets and overlayed on each other. Like scales, they form another layer of skin for you. You begin to understand other beings when you wear a flak jacket for any length of time. Like turtles. Flak jackets aren't comfortable, but any fool knows they are more comfortable than the alternatives.

Just after I get back, my exec and I are talking. While I was on R&R, he'd taken the company out toward Lang Vei and got called back halfway. He didn't get hit, but he knew Charlie was close. He prides himself on staying cool, but that veteran is jacked up. His ass is right up next to his shoulders when we talk. People who don't know better think that you need to get hit to get up. Shit, a lot of times you are more up when you don't get hit but think you are going to be. You are right there, tiptoeing on that motherfucker, the edge. With every step you know you can go over. You don't need to get hit to feel that.

My exec is wide-eyed as hell. Not scared. Just more

like: It's finally, really, really true. "They're here, Skipper, they are fucking here!" he says. We have been seeing signs of them for months now. We have watched it go from nothing to this. What he is telling me is "Bingo!" Fucking bingo!

They tell us that we are surrounded by 4 to 6 divisions of NVA. I believe it. When you're taking as much incoming as we are, when you know that the base at Lang Vei is in NVA hands, you know that you're in very deep shit. This is so serious that images of the Alamo start going through your mind. But this is no John Wayne–Walt Disney bullshit show. At Lang Vei the Green Berets fell in one night.

Lang Vei, the Special Forces base on the Laotian border, fell to NVA in early February. I had visited the place before it was hit, and it was beautifully laid out. I would not have minded having their bunkers and gear. Now, from just a mile from Khe Sanh, Charlie is firing antiaircraft guns on our planes. Our planes are bombing what had once been our fortress at Lang Vei.

Being In and Out of the Game

I watch a Special Forces unit get completely wiped out one day. From on top of an artillery bunker, we view the planned assault. Charlie has dug in on a low ridgeline between Khe Sanh and the Laotian border. Through high-powered binoculars mounted on a tripod, I watch the artillery prep fires. Barrage after barrage, our 105s and 155s churn up the dry dirt on the ridge. After a short silence, helicopters from the coast circle in and land right amongst the gook positions. As soon as the men start

B-52

disembarking from the choppers, Charlie opens up. The sounds of gunfire reach me seconds after the fact. It is just like watching a training exercise, except I can see puffs coming out the mens' backs as they're hit. Dirt is being kicked up from the firing. The helicopters do not lift off; they sit with their rotor blades turning. I watch those brave doggies die trying to attack. After only a few minutes, the survivors climb back on the choppers and leave. You do not win when you try to attack superior firepower that's dug in. Never.

I watch with great fascination, detached from their reality; it is a doggie show. But Charlie brings me into it. Mortar rounds from Charlie start falling on us. My mind flashes: I'm in the game. I'm watching, and I'm in it.

Watching those Green Berets eat it leaves me with a new conviction: Charlie would never overrun us. I sit with a new smug certainty. I had learned a lesson in defense: The man with the home-field advantage is a motherfucker. I wish Charlie would come. I'd love to fight him in here. This fucked-up base called Khe Sanh is ours, not Charlie's—he'll never take us. He has four divisions surrounding us, but Khe Sanh is ours. Charlie doesn't have the firepower or maneuverability that the Marines had in World War II against the Japanese. If you're going to attack fortified positions, you'd better have vastly superior firepower and forces. If you don't, you might as well kiss your sweet ass goodbye.

Yep, I believe we are doing it the right way now. As I impassively watched the Green Berets die, I became a believer. Defense can be a motherfucker. It might not win wars, but it doesn't lose them either.

True, Charlie has the rest of his life to sit out there and peck away at us—he isn't on a one-year tour as we are. There is nowhere else for him to go; he is home. But we have one big-ass advantage over Charlie: Charlie does not have planes at Khe Sanh. He doesn't have bombs, or helicopters, or B-52s.

Yes, he does dump on me. He dumps a lot of rockets, and mortars, and artillery, but I help to bomb his ass. From my patrol reports we plan air strikes. I bomb him through the men who built the bomb, the guy reading a radar screen, and the pilot who drops 'em.

As I watch the doggies call air strikes in on themselves, I know. Come on, Charlie, come on in.

The Man, J.B.

J.B., the colonel, took over the battalion shortly before I took command on the hills. J.B. is almost 20 years in. He had been a platoon commander in Korea. (Most career guys get two wars in the Marines.) At Khe Sanh he has four rifle companies under his command.

I know he cares. I've always been able to see that in men. People who care understand what I mean.

Caring in battle means hurting. J.B. hurts so much when his guys eat it. I see the look in his eyes. I hear it in the slow gentleman's drawl of South Carolina stretched out into the beginnings of a slur as he tells me of the death of the battalion sergeant major.

Our sergeant major was on his third war. He ate a rocket in a command bunker while he was visiting the troops on the trench line. He took it in the head. He was never conscious. Doc told me J.B. kept yelling at the sergeant major, trying to wake him. Like his buddy was just drunk and passed out, J.B. kept trying to wake him.

J.B. has the warmest smile. And his eyes can sparkle. He doesn't bullshit people. He isn't a firebreathing asskicker type like me; he is a guy who gets respect on the strength of his personality. He is very macho and much different from me in his style of macho. My style of macho is an I'll-show-you-how-macho-I-am, young-buck type. J.B. is a man's man. He expects you to respect his shit. He does it by bending over backward to respect yours.

Oh, J.B. kicks my ass a couple of times. I deserve it, too. J.B. knows I am a good man in the bush, though, and he lets me alone in the field. None of this surprise-inspection shit, either. When you command a hill for J.B., it is your kingdom. J.B. calls before he comes up.

One day he wants to take the patrol with my company from Hill 881 South back to Khe Sanh base. He walks in back and doesn't say anything until after we're finished. Then he tells me, "Thank you, it's real heavy bush out there." No critique, nothing. Just thank you.

The entire world as I know it consists only of my battalion. J.B. is The Man of 1st Battalion, 26th Marines. It is that simple. He always acts as if he knows it. He expects everyone else to know it, too, and they all do.

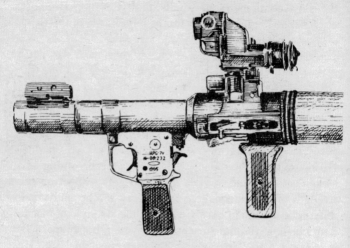

RPG

Fire Fight at the Water Point

Charlie has set up antiaircraft positions just outside our wire on the northern side of the airfield. Incoming flights are receiving regular fire when over the airstrip. Only the medevac choppers land regularly. The medevacs come and depart constantly, like limos pulling in at the hospital. Like the hospital is an auditorium, and guys are leaving the concert in limos. Knock-out show.

Charlie has moved onto a small plateau near our water point, which lies just outside our wire. This northern part of the base is defended by C Company from my battalion. We pump our water from an undefended pond beyond our wire. I always wait for someone else to drink first.

If I were Charlie, I'd fuck with the water. If I were

138

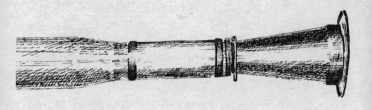

given a shot at Charlie's water, I'd make every guy who had just been on R&R soak his dick in it. I'd poison the dinks if I had a chance. Give me this morality shit? It's being taken out that's the morality. How doesn't count a rat's-ass worth. I've seen guys die, die so hard, so bad, they would have taken a nuke if given a choice. You're missing the point if you think that the morality is in the how. It's irrelevant how you do it or get it done to you.

Regiment orders a platoon-sized search-and-destroy mission on the plateau. They choose Delta Company, and I pick 2nd Platoon. The entire plateau is only 600 meters long. I wait in my bunker, in radio contact with the lieutenant of 2nd Platoon.

Only minutes after starting, the platoon gets hit. RPG—a rocket-propelled grenade—a B-40. The lieutenant's first report is brief: "Contact, point!" As usual, the assistant S-3 from battalion requests a report almost instantly. I sit and say nothing.

The lieutenant of 2nd Platoon is new. A real cocky, macho, South Boston kid. Right from the beginning he calls me Skip. He's fresh out of Basic School and hotter than a popcorn fart.

Again the lieutenant speaks. He's freaked. His voice is three octaves up. He wants a dustoff right now. Got one guy done real fucking bad. I can hear the shooting.

I ask him, "You still taking?"

"We got something going with the one who hit us," he says. I hear grenades exploding and rifle fire over the radio as he speaks. "I need a dustoff, now!" More explosions. "Right now, goddamn it! Do you hear me?" He is screaming at me. "My guy's real, real bad."

As soon as the hiss of the open mike comes on, I press the button on the side of the handset. Speaking deliberately and slowly I say, "OK . . . listen to me . . . listen to me. I don't care what else happens, you hang on. You hang on. You have got to hold it together. Hear me?"

A brief hiss from his open mike. Then:"Roger, 6."

"OK," I'm saying, "you carry him in. You're right outside the wire. It's faster than a chopper."

Behind me I hear the battalion radio net telling the hospital to send an ambulance to the wire at the water point. A short time passes. The lieutenant calls again. He's got a couple of others slightly wounded from that one rocket. They've killed two gooks and the one who fired the RPG is critically wounded by a grenade. Pressing the green rubber-covered button again, I say, "Delta 2, this is 6. They want anyone who is alive to be brought in, copy?"

"The gook ain't going to make it, 6. He ate most of a grenade."

"If he's alive, you bring him in. You copy?"

"Roger, 6."

For most of a minute the mike hisses like a tire going flat.

"6, this is 2."

"This is 6, go ahead."

"We're coming in. The gook is a flunk. Over."

"Roger, 2. 6 out," I answer softly.

I tell one of my radio operators to check on the wounded. When he returns he tells me that the two wounded aren't so bad. I ask him how the point died. He doesn't say a word. He just contorts himself while standing in front of me, arms twisting, fingers grotesquely curled, his face in a mock scream. A whole play, a 2-second death. No words necessary.

After a man's been in a fire fight, his eyes light up, then they slowly darken and sink back into his head. By the time the lieutenant and I meet, he is fast sinking into his sockets. His jowls seem heavy as he speaks, his eyes are glazed. With minimum details he recounts the ambush. Charlie was dug in and popped him first. His guys moved well, he says. No talking, just dumping. His guys really unloaded, just like in training. "I didn't even have to tell 'em," he said, "They just went at 'em." We are alone near the entrance to my bunker.

He starts to leave, then pauses. He says in a hushed tone, "Skip, I did the gook myself. I did him right between his eyes with my pistol. He never would have made it, Skip. I did the gook myself." The lieutenant's eyes are so sad.

Good sign, I'm thinking, not the type to lay bad shit off on somebody else. Welcome to the war, macho man. With that blank look of mine, I say, "You did what you had to do, is all. You did what you had to do. You did real good. Real good."

I can teach guys how to play macho by now; I have become a teacher. If I had tried to comfort him, I would have ruined him, ruined him for war.

As I walk into J.B.'s quarters, also the S-3 situation room, I can feel the sense of vengeance. Old-fashioned Marine Corps vengeance. J.B. is the first to speak.

"You want them?" His eyes are like those of a coach asking his player. He is looking at me.

"I can take them out, Colonel. I will take them out." We stand for a moment staring into one another's eyes. "We're up. I'm up, ready."

After the briefing the air officer walks over and says how great I had been on the radio. How cool, how I had calmed the lieutenant right down. With the same blank look on my face, I say, "I was in my bunker. He was taking it. Talking in a bunker ain't shit."

Tomorrow I'll see whether I am just talking.

Plateau Sweep

There is not much room for creativity. With the plateau my restricted area of operation, it would be like a bird shoot. Ol' boys in regiment do like to panic. To put an entire company of Marines on that small plateau is redundancy personified. It's a good thing we are understrength, or we would trip over one another. I hope to trick Charlie by having 2nd Platoon leave the base at the water point while 1st and 3rd Platoons leave the wire at the other end of the runway. We will sweep outward across the plateau unless it is foggy in the morning. Fog will dictate.

I am ravenous that night. I eat two meals of Cs. I wait and check throughout the evening until the fog comes in, a nice thick fog. I sleep for several hours. Like a child on Christmas Eve, I go to sleep with hopes and dreams dancing in my head—my last remembrance is a wish for fog. I believe it will be close in the fog. I want to do it close. I want to see them. I hope the fog lasts tomorrow.

There is a nice deep, wet, still fog the next morning. After moving the men in small units to avoid arousing suspicion, I'm with 3rd Platoon. 2nd Platoon moves through the water point and fans out across the top end of the plateau—the place they'd started the day before. Most of the covering on the plateau is chest- to head-high elephant grass. Numerous artillery and bomb hits scar it, leaving gaping wounds of bare earth like the acned face of one lightly bearded. Hidden from direct view from Khe Sanh, a second plateau lies hidden just below the one we will sweep. Beyond the plateaus a steep, deep valley dives almost straight down to the Rao Quan River. We slip quietly out through the openings in the wire. The fog hangs just beyond the trench lines like a veil—full and white. There are unexploded artillery shells scattered about like toys tossed by a bored child. The shells are remnants of the ammo-dump explosion. Charlie got a direct hit on the ammo dump one day, and the artillery shells started cooking off. Now I look down at them—sterile punches that never were.

With the fog holding and continuing to hide the plateau, I tell 1st Platoon to move out and over the east end of the runway and to move below the edge of the plateau. The plateau opens from that point like the tip of an arrow head. 2nd Platoon radios that they are in the assigned blocking position. I stand just beyond the wire at the center of the sickle blade formed by 3rd and 1st Platoons. Sunlight scatters the fog. First in holes, quickly reclosed, and then in large gashes. The fog keeps retreating. It suddenly pulls back out across the plateau, over the lip, and back down into the deep canyon.

Lying in front of me is a large cleared area, an area burned by napalm. The clearing is 60 yards across. Marines stand on either side of me, tense and restlessly waiting to go. We are at the edge. Right fucking there—not a doubt in any man's mind. I stand very still trying to show cool, but my heart is redlining like hell. I can hear it stroking in my ears. I feel every little bump and groove in my arterial system. That blood of mine is cascading through my veins like a river out of control.

We must wait for the tip of the sickle blade to show on the plateau to my right. When the lead squad of 1st Platoon shows on the plateau, we will have boxed Charlie in on three sides. The mountains out beyond the canyon jut above the fog. Clouds of fog rest against the mountains, forming a bridge over the canyon to us. The mountains are scarred by B-52 raids and show their earth, like frosting gouged out of a cake.

I see their heads now, the right tip of the blade. The lead squad and the rest of 1st Platoon step silently onto the plateau. I begin walking straight across the opening without saying a word. Marines begin fanning out around me, pointing their rifles from the hip. Some are moving tentatively in a half crouch, ready to jump in any direction. They are moving too slowly. I want to get through the open space as quickly as possible. Quickening my pace and without a word, I begin waving my left arm, swinging it back to front like a farmer scattering seed in his fields. Walking straight ahead and not looking to either side I move quickly across the opening, waving my men on silently. I know my men will come. They will come with me. Almost rushing now the men surge abreast of me. Like birds darting forward toward the seeds I've scattered, they now know what I want. I want into the brush as quickly as possible. It is still when we enter the grass, the only sound that of trousers scraping. No words.

This is the first time I'm using rock and roll prior to contact. My rifle is on automatic and pointing straight out in front of me at hip level. Left hand on the forward handguard, right hand on the grip and just a finger pull away from making anything in front of the barrel trip the light fantastic. Each man points to an area in front of him. Marines on line. I now glance to my left and right as I walk. My eyes sweep in a wide arch around me. My rifle sways in my arms as I walk and point out my kill zone, rocking left to right with the motion of my eyes, my rhythms.

I am watching the movement of the line. The lieutenants are up and slightly ahead of their men. I am tuned into the picture, but an inner voice keeps reminding me over and over again: If it goes off in front of you, pull the trigger! Before you move or shit yourself, pull the fucking trigger. I have no doubt we will hit. I have come to that point with myself: I know it is there, right there.

It goes off to my right, 50 yards away. To the distinctive pops of an M-16, my head and shoulders jerk to the right. I plant my left foot, my rifle rising to my shoulder. An M-16 sounds so much softer than an AK-47. We hit first. The line has gone down into firing position. More M-16s fire, grenades explode. Dropping to my knee I yell to my company radio, "Ask 1st Platoon which is the best way to cover him."

"They're by the edge. Come straight across," he yells a moment later.

Up, I'm yelling, "Let's go! Let's go straight across, come on!" Intermittent fire. Marines moving, grenades exploding. Everyone goes down when a grenade goes off. "Don't shoot unless you can see 'em," I'm yelling. "There are Marines in there. They're all in there. Don't shoot unless you can see 'em."

I hold my rifle down by my side so I can move quicker. I move into the site now and see a foxhole with a dead gook lying in it. A big machine gun sits next to him. A live gook is lying nearby. A Marine guards him and keeps himself under the sight lines of the gook's friends by lying next to him and pointing his rifle right in the gook's face. I move farther in.

"Grenade!" a Marine screams. I dive straight forward like I'm doing a starting dive into a pool. As soon as my elbows hit, I begin pulling in my hands toward my face. I feel the explosion come across me from behind and to my left. It rocks me, and I instantly feel a sting in the palm of my left hand. A sudden wet runs across my left buttock and hamstring. I'm hit. I can feel the blood. I pump my left leg twice. No pain. I do not want to look down. I rise to my knees and say to my radio man, "Am I hit?"

"You pissed yourself," he says. My canteen on my left hip had taken most of the hit, my flak jacket the rest. I thought the water from my canteen was blood—sure as shit felt that way. A loud ringing is in my left ear as we move on through the enemy position. I move to the edge of the plateau. Foxholes. They lie in a slight natural depression just out of sight of our trench line at the base. NVA in the foxholes have clear fields of vision and—more important—a clear shot at the air approach to the runway.

Shifting sites, I see that Marines to my left are firing down into the lower plateau.

I gaze down at the small tree line that lies hidden in the lower plateau, an ideal shelter. Just as I start to call to the 81mm mortar spotter to fire a mission, a voice behind me gasps, "Oh, shit! Your fucking head!"

My radio operator's eyes are riveted on me. Startled back so suddenly from my study, his words, my turn, his stare are all almost at the same moment of looking behind me over my right shoulder. "Skip, your fucking head!" He motions with one hand darting over his head.

I turn and run to a promontory to my right that gives a better view of the steep hillside. My radio operator runs behind me, chattering at me from a distance of 10 yards. Like a mother hen clucking to her chick he says, "Went right over your head. A rocket. Right over you. You didn't even see it. He almost took your head off. You were standing straight up." My radio operators are always giving me lessons that way, punch line at the end.

Reaching the promontory first, I shoulder my rifle. Looking down the barrel at blurred visions, I pick up forms falling downward through the grasses that drop like a slide before me. While my right eye lines the front post in the center of the rear circle, my left follows the target. The rifle sight is just like a camera mounted on a rifle. Both my eyes are open, working independently. The rifle is jumping in its quick-shot jig. My left hand is firm but not fighting as it guides the jumping rifle to the images. My mouth is half open. It is as though I am merely recording this. Ten shots are fired before full realization of what I am doing comes to me. Up until then it felt like just a movie filmed over the barrel of my rifle. Fully in tune now, I finish my clip. The radio men begin firing off to my right. Marines move over the promontory and down the steep hillside. Everyone is firing. I drop my first clip at my feet and insert another from my right pouch. After several more shots, it is pointless; they are gone. I finish the clip anyway.

As I turn from the cliff, I see Marines at the base standing on top of the bunkers and along the trench line cheering, screaming. I'm in a fucking game, I think. They're watching it live. They all wish they were down here getting some with us, but I'm just in a fucking game. I walk back to the two gooks.

The wounded gook is propped on one elbow. "Corpsman!" I call.

"You don't need the corpsman," says the scruffy Marine guarding him. "He's shot clean through his calf, is all."

The corpsman reports no casualties among us and starts bandaging the wounded NVA's leg, while several other Marines search the dead one. As they empty his pockets, the squad leader takes a Buck knife from his own pocket. In almost one motion he opens the blade, tilts the dead man's chin back, and slits his throat. "Hey!" I yell.

"Just making sure he's dead's all. Don't want him getting some again," wild-eyed and grinning, the squad leader answers.

"Well, don't you take him apart, you hear me!"

Like a scolded dog he turns away and folds his knife. Quickly they unbutton the trousers of the dead man and pull his pants down to reveal his crotch. It's a habit we have, a recent tradition. The rumor is that NVA who are circumcised tend to be officers. Whenever we zap one and get our hands on him, one of our rituals is to drop his trousers and check his pecker. Part of our report is whether he is circumcised or not.

I have the dead man dragged far from where he is killed. His buddies will come looking for him. Let 'em look. When they're out crawling around in the dark looking for their buddies and cussing, it's my payback for all the shit they've been dumping on me.

Even though we are just outside the wire, regiment wants the wounded NVA flown back to the base. The pilot barely lifts off before he puts down again just outside the wire. I'm sure we impress the hell out of the gook, who gets his own helicopter for a 10-second ride.

As we resume the sweep toward 2nd Platoon, the heat of the day becomes relentless. The fear and exhaustion of the fire fight, its taste and smell, are fresh upon me. The grass now seems taller and thicker. My senses are dull and drugged. Too much adrenalin has gone through me; I'm exhausted. Just before joining with 2nd Platoon, we move over the ambush site of yesterday.

One of the dead gooks is still here, unfound during his buddies' search the night before. In their haste the day before 2nd Platoon had not searched this one, who was shot while running away. I know everyone up to LBJ will want to know everything they can about Charlie around Khe Sanh. I tell the chief of scouts to search the gook. The soldier had been so well lit up when the Marines shot him that it is like searching in a vat of worms—not too much is solidly in place. The scout tosses me the man's personal possessions, a look of disgust his only statement.

Winners' Locker Room

An energy hits me after we get back inside our wire. When I am sure that we had finished the sweep without casualties, new life surges into me. I have an arrogant feeling of power. I feel like a superstar walking down the gangway. Striding down Main Street, I walk oblivious to the possible rocket and artillery barrages. The eyes, the faces, the cheers, the shouts of the people who had witnessed the battle line my path into the colonel's quarters. Their fight had been watching a map on the wall or listening to radio transmissions from my company while dreaming their own battle. My presence now before them is the confirmation of their dream. The dream that all of us have been dreaming for so long: payback.

Charlie has become so arrogant that he fucks with our airplanes, our lifelines, our umbilical cords. But the man who killed the shotters has arrived. I carry the NVA machine gun over my shoulder. It is the reality to those Marines' dreams. They now see that it is true. I stride down the stairs to the battalion headquarters bunker.

J.B.'s eyes hold his smile, his relief, his happiness, his joy. One of his men had done it; got Charlie and walked away. J.B. is very pleased that the men showed enough class to bring in a live prisoner to tell where others might be. Everyone wants at Charlie.

J.B. pumps my hand while holding it with both of his. He breaks out his bottle of Jack Daniels. Empty C-ration cookie cans serve as glasses. Toasts are offered to Delta Company by J.B. and the other staff officers. My toast is to my man who was killed the day before.

"What don't you know?" I ask. I know that during contact my battalion radio operator had given his usual excellent running commentary. He is as good as any play-by-play announcer. "Oh," I say while looking over at the assistant S-3 and holding up two fingers, "we returned fire. Even me, Major. Two clips."

There are two facts that I omit reporting to battalion. I don't tell them that the gook's machine gun had misfired. The guy who burned the gook gunner was saved by a misfire. I also don't tell them about thinking I was hit in the leg or about the shrapnel in my left hand. I'll be fucked if the only friendly wounded that day is me.

The Scouts

In the mountains near Laos live the Bru, a Montagnard people. As far as the Vietnamese are concerned, the Montagnards have about as many rights as a black did in Alabama in 1900. The Vietnamese, it seems, are not the most tolerant people on the planet.

The Bru are like a separate nation. They are a gentle, laughing people. I have two who are Kit Carson scouts. They are former Vietcong soldiers who have defected to the South Vietnamese side. Lot and Quong are their names. Lot is brave, fun loving, and intelligent. He plays the bamboo flute. Quong is funny, into eating, and a coward. He is addicted to pussy, and he spends all his money on it. Quong's favorite song—of his own invention, I think—is about fucking continuously. Interspersed with the few words are cries and hoots of delight.

As Charlie closes in and the siege starts, the scouts lose all contact with the mountain villages. Ol' Quong is really hurting. He comes to see me with the chief of scouts, and it takes all the courage Quong has. If it were not so important, Quong would never dare talk to me. As far as he is concerned, I am the closest thing to a king that he will ever know. Through the chief scout he humbly begs me to help him. His dick is dying, he believes. He hasn't had any pussy in so long that he believes that his dick is actually dying.

"What the fuck does he want me to do, jerk him off?" I laugh.

Everyone has their superstitions, don't they?

Outhouse Goddess

Reporters are curious motherfuckers. During the first few weeks of the siege, every reporter in Nam tries to put in an appearance. Barrages are an effective treatment for curiosity, though. One string of incoming and they are usually game for the next flight out.

A beautiful, petite German woman arrives. She is a photographer, I think. She stays at the base hospital, which we call Charlie Med. One of my men, a Mexican dude, is being treated at Charlie Med for shrapnel wounds while she is there. When he is released, he rushes back to give me the exciting news. Several of us are standing in the trench line sunning ourselves when he approaches.

"Check eet out, Skeepper," he says excitedly. "I'm een the four-hole sheeter at Charlie Med taking a sheet, right? Before I know what is goen on, thees chick walks in. I swear to God, Skeepper, let Him strike me down. I ain't bullsheetting you." He's almost jumping up and down. His arms flail. "She drops her pants and seets on a sheeter next to me and starts rapping, asking me where I'm from. Man, I doan know whether to look at her pussay or look her een the eyes while she's talking, you know? Eet blows my mind, man. I hear her dropping, her sheet starts coming out."

"What the fuck did you expect," I say, "mariachi music?"

"I mean, I'm blown away! I can't beleeve it," he says. "She's beautiful, man. I'll never eet pussay that fine. All I get to do in Nam is sheet with it."

Guys are like sharks. As soon as they smell blood, there's a feeding frenzy.

"Hey, did you stick your head down in there and smell her shit after she left?" one of the listeners pipes in.

"Might as well have, he didn't get to sniff her pussy," another says.

"You mowtherfuckers just jealous 'cause I at least seen the pussay." He is trying to defend himself.

"Yeah?" a guy says, "When you jerk off, you going to be thinking of her pussy or her asshole?"

The Mexican's moment of triumph is shot down in flames, the laughter and howls pelting him as he walks away.

The Doomed Patrol

February 1968. Bravo Company had been taking a beating from incoming mortars. A reinforced 29-man patrol left the wire on February 25 to locate the NVA position. Charlie gave them three as bait—three unarmed NVA walking up the road, seemingly oblivious to the patrol. Bravo closed in to take prisoners and stepped between the two ends of a curved bunker line. *Newsweek* magazine called it the Doomed Patrol.

I heard the whole thing on the radio. After Bravo

took four casualties, I recommended that they get their dead and get out. They tried to fight. Attack.

Bravo sent out another platoon to assist. It got chewed up by concentrated mortar fire from Charlie. Marines died trying to save dying Marines. That is our way. It separates us from everyone else. A Marine likes to know that someone will try to get to him if he's down and can't get himself out. That's what Bravo Company tried. But they couldn't get most of the guys.

The lieutenant of the patrol and most of his men were killed. One of the men was captured.

After hearing the radio reports from the patrol and the backup platoon, we know only that we have taken a big hit and that we are still taking. Charlie is now sending mortar fire inside the wire. It is as though we are walking through a tunnel. J.B. and I are out in the open, jumping over the trench lines, but the doom that hangs around us forms a tunnel that encloses and guides us to the spectacle of the slaughter still going on.

Bravo's command bunker overlooks the entire scene. It is barren, desolate terrain—red dirt with mortars hitting. Marines carrying others, dragging, crawling. This is a live show. This is no Hollywood epic. This is the real thing. Those are Marines getting hit.

Bravo's CO, Ken, had taken over the company only a few months before. Before commanding Bravo, Ken was CO of Headquarters and Services Company, the largest unit in the battalion. But it was a staff job, not line.

As Ken looks back at J.B. and me, his face seems like a mask that is melting. The sorrow flows from his eyes in dry tears that seem to pass out and over his cheeks and chin like wax running down a candle. We stand together beside his bunker as the wounded stream in.

J.B. is crushed. Like a coach who knows the game's over. His Marines acted like Marines, but they lost one. Big.

J.B. says to me, "Well, Ernie, let's go see the Old Man." We walk out in the open, striding. Oblivious to possible incoming. In the dark, together and alone.

Regimental CO is where he always seems to be. In his bunker. It is the old French bunker. Khe Sanh has a lot of tradition. As superstitious as this guy is, I can just imagine the tripping out he does on that.

J.B. runs down the facts for the CO. Bravo has lost almost two thirds of its men. Most of one platoon is left out there, status unknown. Relatives of the missing will be told in 24 hours. In 24 hours the world will know—there are reporters at the trench line.

J.B. asks to go out to get his men. Regimental CO tells J.B. that the battalion is needed to defend the airstrip. He is right.

J.B., the CO, and I are seated in a small circle on green folding stools. J.B. says, "Well, I know how these things go. I'm prepared to take the fall for this one." The patrol leader was a new 2nd lieutenant, the lowest-ranking officer. J.B. will take the rap for the Doomed Patrol.

Top Man pays in our game. If you're a Marine, that's the way it is. To have the glory we seek, we have to be willing to pay the price. I see J.B. pay that day. Like a shotgun blast in his face. In the Marine Corps if it ever comes your turn, you take it. That is macho. When we listened to the lieutenant die on the radio, we knew it was J.B.'s turn. Who gives a fuck whether it was his fault or not? You want to be in command? You pay. That's what leaders are for. Not just the wins.

The regimental CO just pats J.B. on his knee and tells him not to worry about it.

Two weeks later J.B. is transferred and becomes the exec of the 4th Marines.

The new CO of 1/26 is the former S-4 of the regiment.

The Warrior System

Warriors must be a tribe or nation of people. From the dead souls of warriors past we evolve to pass our eternal march through time as soldiers. My tribe recognizes each other through their eyes. The leaders are old men in their eyes. The young ones look to the old men for guidance.

In the warrior's system you work your way back, low man in front. Maybe back in the world you try to get ahead, but not where we are. What we men with the old eyes do is kick the young men's asses to move them forward—to possibly get their asses killed when they feel much safer in lying down. The voice of survival is yelling in their ears, "Turn around, boy, and get your C-ration-eating ass outta this." It is up to us old men to teach them by moving them up, by forcing them forward. The training of the Marine is to ignore that inner voice of survival speaking—to move when one of the old men shows you how to move forward by being with you, yelling at you, and kicking your ass. That's how my tribe of warriors evolved, as ass kickers.

We line warriors have one advantage over the rest of the world: We can purge the tribe. If one of us betrays the tribe, we can take care of it.

All the casualties we are taking are breaking J.B.'s

heart. Anyone can see it. But it seems to me that the regimental CO and our exec are blind to everything except themselves. As far as I know, that exec never spends one night outside the wire. During the siege he stays away from me—fortunately for him. I will kill him if I just get the chance.

I check his bunker out. He always has a radio man or someone down there with him. I would do him if he were alone. I would put a grenade down his bunker. I would pull the pin, let the spring handle go, count to 2, and roll it down on him. This is not one of my dreams; I think about it wide-ass awake.

I have no feelings like that about doing Charlie. Don't get me wrong. I do Charlie every chance I get. But I respect Charlie. I don't hate him. I hate that major.

Shit, I would have no problem doing him right in his face. Let him see it, then zap him. In my view that major is not on our side; that chicken shit is on his own. He is assigned to my battalion—my tribe—but he isn't one of us. No fucking way.

The Boys of Graves Registration

I see the dead. None of them look like they belong there.

Guys from graves registration do the dead for their job. Graves registration is right near my bunker at Khe Sanh. It is just a tent in the beginning, but business gets real good—booming after a while.

After the guys do the NVA who got shot while spying outside the wire, the guys from graves try to prop up what is left so they can take pictures. They have the NVA leaning up against boxes like a bunch of Raggedy Ann dolls. All floppy. When someone's got that many holes in 'em, they won't stay up. Bones are all broken. This dude from graves reminds me of a photographer doing a still-life shot. Just working a bowl of fruit. Those gooks are about as real to that guy as a still life.

Guys from graves have the most alive eyes I've ever seen. Maybe they have me hypnotized. Those guys from graves are not from my planet.

THE SIEGE: SHUTTING DOWN

Waiting for the Axeman

Did you ever wonder what the guy standing in front of the firing squad feels like? How about the guy who is going to get electrocuted, or hung, or drawn and quartered, or boiled, or burned, or buried, or skinned alive? Those of us at Khe Sanh during the siege have some idea. The soldier at Khe Sanh is the guy waiting for the axeman to strike. We wait day after day, week after week. There is nothing to do but hole up, suck in, and wait. Am I going to get hit during this string of incoming or not? My tour isn't up until June. Five more months of this shit?

Khe Sanh is the biggest news event going. Back in the world it's in all the magazines and papers and on TV every night. Every night the announcers tell how many rounds we had taken the day before. The Marines are cut off and taking a hell of a pounding. President Johnson has a scale model of our base in the White House.

When the siege starts we are being hit from everywhere, it seems. Long-range artillery pounds us from 12 miles

122mm Rocket Launcher

away in Laos. The 122mm rockets screech in on us from Hill 881 North.

We listen in awe to air strikes that are called on Charlie. By the second week of February, six B-52s bomb the North Vietnamese every 3 hours, day and night. If you like watching ordnance go off—it is like fireworks—a B-52 strike can pop your nuts. And there are more than the B-52s. One day close to 800 planes route over Khe Sanh to dump on Charlie. After a while we can't count them anymore, though. When the monsoon fog closes in and stays in, we can't count on anything.

The fog, the night, the jungle—they all make counting hard. Word is that there are six thousand of us and forty thousand of them. Who can tell? All we know is that each morning the NVA trench line is a little closer to our wire.

The Marine Corps had done nothing to prepare us for sustained bombardment. We think that any day we'll break out of the wire and kick the fuck out of Charlie. No one thinks that we will just sit there and take it for 77 days.

One guy down at battalion headquarters makes a ritual of keeping his personal calendar. It is a ceremony for him to tear out a page every morning. I tear a month out when he isn't looking. He goes berserk.

Bunkers

There are two kinds of bunkers at Khe Sanh: pre-January 1968 and post-January 1968. Before the siege we might dig down several feet before building, but the sides of most bunkers are above ground.

During the siege the guys go on a rat trip. The entrance to a siege bunker is a slanted hole 3 feet in diameter. The passage goes down 4 feet and opens into a den. Inside the entrance is a passage with a sandbag blast wall at the end. For blast protection you never want to have a straight opening into your bunker. No cheap shots in. My bed is sometimes a cot, most times a stretcher.

Topsoil, the blonde kid whose hair grows through a patina of dirt, lives in an underground bunker on Hill 881. He proudly shows it to me. His is a little different. He has a storage room built off the main den and hundreds and hundreds of cans of C rations in the storage room. "I'll never starve, Skipper," he giggles. He can stay down there for two tours.

We always ate in our bunkers, but bunker etiquette changes as the siege continues. Presiege you didn't shave or brush your teeth in your bunker. Once the siege starts you do everything in your bunker, including pissing. You use a 105mm artillery casing as a chamberpot unless the rocket barrage is such that you go right in your pants. Before the siege talking was a favorite pastime. It sealed your relationship with men. You'd be hunched over a low stool late at night, a hissing lantern flickering, shadows dancing against the sandbags. He told of his past, his dreams, and his beliefs. You listened, seeking to know another man—someone you'd never see again after this time. During the siege there is nothing to say. We all are aware of what is happening to us. It is like standing with your hands down at your sides while someone's unloading you. What is there to say?

During the first weeks of the siege we always check any bunker that gets hit. We try to figure out what could have been done to make it stronger. We check over and over again, trying to find one that can take it. Our new supply officer, a 1st lieutenant, builds one he thinks might make it. It has what amounts to a double roof. The first is meant to set off the blast and the second to provide protection for the men inside. For supports he uses a lot of wooden timbers that he finagled out of the Seabees. Charlie tests his design with a rocket. It is close, but no cigar. The blast does not penetrate his bunker, but it does collapse the roof. The lieutenant dies when his neck breaks.

Everyone's got a pet, and I think that lieutenant was J.B.'s. J.B. stops at my area on his way back from visiting the collapsed bunker. When macho says that you don't cry, emotions take their revenge in your face. J.B.'s is almost puffy. His eyes have a red tint at the edges of the lids, just where they touch the eyeball.

"They thought they heard him for a while. It took about 5 minutes to get in. The men swear they heard him screaming, but the doc says his neck broke and that he died instantly. I don't know, Ernie, I just hope he didn't suffer."

With a deep sigh J.B. shrugs and pats me on my flak-jacketed shoulder. "I wish there were something we could do—anything but this." He turns without expecting an answer and leaves.

Pet Doggie

The doggies get a new communications officer, a 1st lieutenant straight from stateside. This doggie is totally enthralled with real field Marines. He visits every day and always brings gifts—things for us to eat. The doggie does not know about our tradition of eating alone, but we all welcome him. He is such a nice doggie. He is like some young guy on a street corner back in the world who suddenly gets to hang around with the street gang.

He comes to my bunker one morning and asks me and my officers to join him in the trench line next to the executive officer's bunker. He brings us a feast of shrimp. The shrimp had been dehydrated and packed in a gallon-sized green number 10 can. He had reboiled them, and he had made cocktail sauce from ketchup and Tabasco and who knows what else. Doggies have everything.

Grimy hands. Dirty, shitty, filthy hands grab shrimp and dip them into the sauce. The doggie does not eat. He watches us instead. The officers and the gentlemen are out for the day; the scumbags and hoboes are in. Reaching in, dipping, chomping. Suck-your-fingers good. The stuff is as good as pussy.

A day or two later I am on the other side of the base discussing avenues of approach from my area. Two rockets chug over us like freight trains. I crouch with the assistant S-3 as they hit.

"They got you," he says.

"Bullshit. They hit the doggies."

We complete the inspection of the line before I walk back to my area. Forty minutes have passed since the two rockets had hit the main army bunker. The bodies of four guys lie next to the shattered bunker. They are rolled in ponchos, and the lower part of their legs and their boots are showing. It reminds me of cigars, the way they are rolled up.

"I think we got 'em all," one Marine is saying. "What a fucking mess. I feel like a fucking butcher, handling all that meat."

I gaze at the lifeless forms for a moment, turn, and walk back to my bunker.

I sit on my stool and undo my web belt. "You see him, George?" I ask my radio operator.

"The doggie lieutenant? Yup, all hamburger. Waist down he was fine, but all the rest was red gooey hamburger." He speaks rapidly as though he can hardly wait to end his task.

Our eyes meet. For only a moment I see sadness in his eyes. Then an almost impish grin is on his face. He will not let this get to him.

Just like George, my company exec is one of the coolest cucumbers around. But he had adopted that doggie like a puppy. I have never seen him so upset.

"Goddamn it, Skipper. Goddamn it, he shouldn't have died." His words seem so out of place. "I'm going to write to his wife." He looks to me for reassurance and approval.

"What are you going to tell her, Lieutenant? That her husband is a hamburger sandwich?"

"But he was a great guy. A first-class guy." He is almost choking.

"Leave it be. Let her have her own dreams of him the way she wanted him to be."

That doggie was just doing his job, like the rest of us. The world's loss.

Officer's Macho

Every day, either when going to or returning from the morning meeting at the command bunker, I am shelled. Sometimes I get it coming and going. "They want me. It's just me that they want," I tell my radio operators. "I go down the main road. Bam! I come up the trench line by the garbage dump. Bam! Fuckers have some kind of homing device planted in my ass. They just watch a receiver for when I move. They're getting me bracketed."

In the first few weeks of the siege, company commanders and the battalion commander continue standing in the command bunker during a barrage. We are cool. Charles wasn't going to interrupt our morning briefing.

Nobody plays more macho than Marine Corps officers. Only cool, ice macho counts with us. Expressionless eyes. Passion is not a desirable trait in a Marine officer. Emotions kill.

But Khe Sanh is a bitch who does things her way with you. We go from meeting like that, standing, to where it is perfectly appropriate to sit your ass down any place you want to. You can go down or under anything when a barrage starts. After more time passes, we don't even bother with meetings.

Life Underground

Imagine 30 men in an underground bunker with not much more than a thousand square feet of space for all of them. Subtract from this the space occupied by the sandbag walls used to create separate bunkers within the bunker. The only ventilation is from two tunnels. Lighting is provided by kerosene, white-gas lanterns, or candles. Imagine living there for over 2½ months solid with no weekends away at the cabin.

I read with glee an interview with a doggie general who came to Khe Sanh. He said words to the effect that he was utterly shocked at the filth. "The place was not policed," he said indignantly. *Police* means not just clean; it means polished.

I'd like to have seen that doggie come by in his shower cap saying, "Where are the showers?" One incoming barrage, and he would have taken his shower cap right off. Filth is the least of our problems.

Rats

There were always rats at Khe Sanh. Not your stereotypical Asian variety of chopstick-using rat. Khe Sanh rats are snarling gray suckers with big heads. Having evolved in a jungle environment, those rats are capable of fighting anything.

The garbage dump set off their population explosion. The dump is in a narrow gully just outside the south side of the base. Before the siege the rats had to stand in line to take their shot; a garbage dump in Vietnam is the trendiest restaurant around as far as the natives are concerned. How disgusting to watch the Montagnards—a beautiful, gentle people—slogging around in our slop. With empty sandbags over their shoulders, they would diligently pick through the dump every day. They would swarm around and over any vehicle taking out a fresh load. Our garbage is the best we had to offer to those we are there to save.

The rats begin exerting themselves several breeding cycles into the siege. A rat jumps on my chest one night. On my back on my cot, I slap at him with my left hand while I try to shield my face with my right. He is grinning at me, I swear.

Rats love the sandbag walls. Since the walls are several layers thick, the rats have a lot of room for their quarters. You can hear them in there screaming, eating, fucking, and kicking each others' asses. Rats are nasty—they are always fighting.

Rats behave more logically during the siege than we do. They let their feelings out. You can hear them squeaking and going berserk during a barrage. Us macho men just sit there quietly and take it.

Constipation

The mind can fuck up any part of the body. As the siege continues my mind says, "Now, Ernest, Vietnam is very serious. And just to remind you of how serious it is,

I'm going to plug your asshole. You can do whatever you want with the rest of yourself, but the asshole is mine."

After a while I can only eat what the asshole will let out. There is a direct correlation between what is happening and how often my asshole becomes unplugged—fiber has nothing to do with it. During the siege a shit is like going and having your hair done. Something you really look forward to. Except your appointment is determined by your brain releasing your muscles. It is that big a deal.

Trenches

It takes a special event like a shit to get you out of your bunker. That's how trenches develop—because we need to get around. We always had them around the perimeter of the base, but after the siege starts we even dig them to the shitters. Then we move the shitters underground. The trench lines at Khe Sanh evolve that way, in an as-needed fashion. Like the windshield on a car that is hit and cracks to create a random design, the trenches at Khe Sanh spread in confusing grids and interlocking mazes.

Resupply

At the beginning of the siege regular resupply flights stop landing. Instead, a plane with rollers on the floor of the cargo bay taxis on the air strip, drops the rear ramp, jettisons the supplies, and takes off without stopping. The supplies are strapped to aluminum sleds. After unloading the sleds the Air Force stacks them near the unloading area in a slight hollow.

The Marines have quickly expanded the base by five times the manpower, but our supplies of building material never catch up. We have nothing to build our bunkers with other than what we can beg, borrow, or steal. Even sandbags are a rare item for a while. We never steal material from each other, but if someone's bunker takes a hit while they are in it, we use the best parts of what is left. Superstition is a luxury that we can't afford.

My company area is just over the rise from the unloading point where the Air Force stacks the aluminum sleds. Once the men discover the metal pallets, it is Loot City. Whenever an airman objects, they tell him to go fuck himself.

Those aluminum sleds make excellent roofing material. You can dig a 4- to 5-foot-square hole, put one of those mothers on top, and not need any other supports. If you put five or six layers of sandbags over and around it, you can stop up to an 82mm mortar round. (Nothing we build stops a direct hit from a rocket or arty round.)

It is mid morning when a scruffy little Marine comes crawling down the tunnel to my bunker. "Hey, Skipper, some Air Force dude wants ta see ya. I figger he's pissed off about the pallets we bin stealin'." Panting, he kneels there at the entrance as though one word from me would provide the answer to our dilemma.

"Kissss . . . myyy . . . assss," I sing in a rising inflection. I am seated in trousers and boots, just my dog tags and glasses above the waist. After slipping into a flak jacket and donning my piss pot, I crawl up the tunnel entrance.

As I kneel there in the trench, I look up into the bright blue sky. Towering over me on top of the line looms someone standing like Patton with his legs apart.

The brightness of the sudden sunlight blinds me; I can see no more than his shadowy outline. As I stand up, my face comes to his knees.

My sleeveless flak jacket hangs from my skinny shoulders, unzipped. My trousers are almost black with grime—and crackly. My boots hang outward from my ankles untied, slipped on for lounging. As I blink again and again, his appearance comes into focus. He is an Air Force lieutenant colonel—same rank as J.B. He's wearing tight-fitted utilities, fresh and clean. A clean shoulder holster with a .45-caliber pistol crosses his chest. What sets me off is his hat. It's one of those silly-assed ball-cap types. Swear to God! Baseball cap with the big silver oakleaf, the insignia of his rank, pinned to the front. It is clear that this motherfucker has just arrived.

I have never seen an Air Force guy who looks military to me. I always figure that if shit gets really bad and we have to send the Girl Scouts into battle, we can use the Air Force to cover for them on the cookie sales.

"Who in the hell is in charge here!" he barks down at me. "What's your rank?"

Bingo! He had hit my magic button.

"I'm, oh my goodness, I'm a lieutenant, sir." My face starts swaying as I limply bring my hand to my face.

"Well, what do you do?" he growls, sure now that he is in complete control.

"I'm in charge of this show troop. And . . . and we got caught here during one of our shows. We really don't belong here. As you can see, I'm a nervous wreck." I'm all the way into my homo trip by now. That jerk is so dumb, he thinks I'm serious.

"I want all my equipment returned right now. You got that, Lieutenant?"

With fingers slightly parted, I bring my hand to the tip of my helmet in another limp salute. "Yes, sir," I lisp. I have not saluted anyone in a long time. Marines don't salute in the field.

Several men have gathered in the trench and can barely control themselves. Smirks like knife slashes appear across their faces.

"You don't bring 'em, you're not going to get fed," he calls out over his shoulder as he marches away.

One of the guys grabs his own crotch saying, "Feed this!"

I think we'll never see him again. I figure one barrage and he'll understand. Well, nothing hits, and this guy comes back about an hour later. I am outside talking to someone.

"Hey," he yells upon seeing me. "I thought I told you to bring those sleds down."

Looking at him, I straighten up. "You want 'em, go get your boys and come get 'em. You try, and I'm going to do your ass myself."

He jerks, suddenly startled as though given some tragic news. Saying nothing he slowly turns, his head and eyes fixed on me while his body draws him away. I never see him again.

Wonder if he thought I was a dancer? He'd be telling stories like: "Goddamn, those Marines are all crazy and vicious—even their faggot entertainer ones!"

Constant and Random

The guy I am talking to is little, but he is tough as a rhino's ass. Blonde with a crew cut, Corporal Mac is a macho artillery forward observer. Although he is a tough guy, he is also a joker, a yuk-yuk type with happy eyes.

Chatting away and laughing between each sentence, Mac squats at the foot of the tunnel entrance to my bunker. I sit on a folding stool 5 feet away.

With surprise I see Mac suddenly fly toward me. At the same time that I register the impact of his body against my chest, I am aware of the sound of a nearby hit that has sent a rush of wind down the tunnel. Backward we tumble off the stool. It is like taking a clean punch on the chin: no pain, just lights out for a second. When I come to, Mac is kneeling beside me, trying to clear his own head.

"Check your men." My groggy words set a look of panic on Mac's face. A team of Mac's men had been reinforcing the roof of his bunker when the round hit.

A few moments later I hear Mac outside, his voice rolling down the tunnel. His tone carries the despair of the observer. "Skipper! Ohhh, Skipper!"

I reach for my piss pot. I gulp deeply, as though added air will carry me through what's coming.

As I pull myself out of the trench I see the wounded man. His hair is red and curly, and it fits with the freckles on his cheeks. Only his neck and head move. Taut his mouth, the strain of craning his neck so clear. Like a man trying to pull himself over the edge of a cliff, again and again his head rises and falls back. The rest of his body is paralyzed.

His left leg is severed; the lower part of it, in the boot, now lies beside his face. His right leg lies straight down and is shredded like confetti. The white of shattered bone points out beyond red flesh. The scene is turning red, flesh upon a growing pool of blood. My eyes are horrified lenses of red.

"Corpsman! Corpsman!" I scream.

Someone jumps out of the trench behind me. Men rush from all directions. Where is the corpsman?

"Oh God, the corpsman was working on the bunker too. Skipper, he was with them."

I scream the corpsman's name over and over. We run in expanding circles, Mac and I, screaming the corpsman's name. We search for a few seconds that are a lifetime.

The missing corpsman appears. He had been in the shitter and crawled to a nearby bunker after the round hit.

"I was afraid there'd be more." A look of sorrow and shame is on his face.

"Forget it."

As we speak, others gather to tend the wounded man. They hide him from my view.

I notice how blue the sky is.

After they take him to Charlie Med, I kneel at the small blackened crater beside which he had lain. You can tell from a crater from which direction the round came. The crater points to one of our 105mm artillery batteries, which is nearby. Had it been a short round? Who cares? What difference does it make who gets the credit?

At Khe Sanh artillery is constant and random. That's what I hate about artillery. It's so impersonal.

Sound

You avert your eyes instinctively when shit goes off, but you cannot hide from sound. The sound invades your being. Jesus Christ, it's like someone blowing sound up your ass and nose, through your ears, into your eyes, and down your throat. During a heavy string of incoming, when you're down in your bunker, the sound of incoming is a shock wave that comes right through the ground from all sides, including top and bottom. Boom!

You learn to distinguish the size and type of hit by the sonic boom. 61mm mortar is a jab of a sound, unless it's right over you. An 82mm mortar jolts you. The 152mm shots from Co Roc seem to lift the entire bunker and slam it down again. The sound is so great that it ceases to be perceived as just sound. It is concussion. Too many shots in a row and you go out just like a guy who's down on the ropes.

Despite all the sound of battle, however, the human sound always seems to get through—the screams of a guy going out badly. Your ears are always so wide open when it happens. Those screams etch themselves like unwanted grooves on a record, forever dominating memory.

Anticipation

There is no circulation in our bunkers. Just the smells of kerosene, gas, and cigarettes. Coughing. Filth. But when I think Charlie is coming in, I can breathe again. He is on the wire and coming. Boy, am I alive.

If we can't go out, let him come in. I want him to come. I have armed myself with an M-14 rifle with a full automatic selector. I tape two clips together bottom to bottom so I can get 40 shots instead of just 20. I choose a corpsman's hipsack and load it with about a dozen double clips.

I can kick a lot of ass with that shit. My firing position is a tiny bunker on top of the battalion bunker. It is sand-bagged in. I think Charlie will come right down the runway. This is where my position faces. I would have the advantage

175mm M-107

Charlie always had on us. When Charlie hit us from ambush, he was always dug in. He was a low, small target, and he knew where we were. This time it would be different.

Charlie has other plans. The hardest he hits our wire is in front of the ARVN Rangers one night. The Rangers go into Charlie's trench line. The ARVN lieutenant is wounded and cut off from his men. They are trying to rescue him. He waves them off. The dude sucks his pistol and pulls the trigger. That is macho. Ultimate macho. He had ceased to be an effective leader. He was a liability to his men, so he took himself out.

Macho is not just about winning. You play by the rules, or you ain't playing. That lieutenant had balls. I don't know if I could be that brave.

We hit Charlie with everything we have. All the mortars and artillery at Khe Sanh and 175mm artillery from the coast. It is a light show. Puff the Magic Dragon gunships are pissing red bullets onto Charlie, and every fifth round is a red tracer. Those gunships put out so much so fast that it looks like a stream of red piss. The sound of the Gatling guns is like a bad case of diarrhea.

I imagine Charlie down there that night. He's getting mortared and hit by artillery, and gunships are nailing him from above. He keeps trying to attack through all that. Shit, I am a dreamer. I'm hoping I get a crack at Charlie, but he never gets over the wire. I never get off a shot that night.

Beauty and the Bomb

Despite my focus, my concentration on survival, the beauty of the mountains burns through. It can burn such a deep hole in you.

I remember the beauty as I watch a B-52 approach a ridgeline across from Khe Sanh. An area I had patrolled. The planes fly from my left to my right, 18,000 feet up. I am not thinking of Charlie or the war as I watch. I think of the place I had once known, the beautiful forest there on that ridge. As the bombs hit, the ridgeline blooms before my eyes, left to right, in a puff of gray smoke. Just as suddenly, the blossoms fold downward. Earth and trees fall as fast as they had opened a moment before. The booming vibrations now pass by me, shocking me back to where I am.

If war is life, then bombs are religion. Bombs are religion because they can bring you right to the essence of existence. Any guy who gets caught in the depth or radius of an exploding bomb gets religion immediately. War religion.

I see what the bomb ceremony does to Charlie. I laugh my ass off when I hear about NVA officials mocking the effectiveness of American bombing. If our bombs aren't effective on Charlie, then there are a whole lot of dead motherfuckers from someplace else out there. I see them and smell them rotting. I am a witness for those big Kahunas, the B-52s. Saturation religion. Baby, I believe!

I watch Charlie get baptized one day. Skyhawk fighter bombers are going to do a bombing run on Charlie's trench lines at the east end of the airfield. Our air officer and I go outside to see. We are 300 to 400 meters away from the line.

Skyhawks can almost dance. A clear sky reflects off metal points that glisten as the plane swoops up, and then effortlessly slants left. Just like its namesake, it swoops in and turns before diving. This is to be a kill, a ritual saved for the most profound effect. Bombs free, falling free.

Fins, the stabilizers, open to slow the descending ceremony. Rifle fire, AK-47 on full automatic. The plane pulls
up, then off to the right. Back up and away it flies, back
toward the coast. A faceless god who flies straight back to
the air-conditioned bar.

The earth rises up and outward as the first bomb
explodes. Then several more flash, and earth is thrown
upward. Pushed upward and blooming like large flowers.

I see a figure emerge through the dirt. From a blos-
som 60 feet up, a figure emerges. It is upside down and
begins to twirl and tumble while rising upward. No sound.
An arm leaves the form and spins off on its own journey
upward. Then a leg joins the arm and breaks away on its
own.

Whacking sounds near me send me into an instinctive
downward move. Shrapnel from the same bombs is hitting
the sandbags next to me, a kiss blown to us from the
plane. Crouching, I watch the form and his pieces silently
fall back to earth. What a defiant man, firing away as he
was taken out, watching himself being taken out.

We are cheering, the other officer and I. While the
guy fell back to the earth, we cheer just like we are
watching a ball go through the uprights. Anticipation,
realization, elation. Cheering because we don't just take,
we give too. That airdale is proud. Proud as though he had
gotten to fuck the guy himself. He is with that pilot who
dropped on Charlie. My association with airdales isn't as
close as the air officer's, but I cheer too. Anyone can have
a piece of Charlie as far as I am concerned.

Outgoing Arty

Outgoing artillery is like scanning a newspaper and listening to music at the same time. It is like reading a paper and just passing time. You scan the paper, but you are not really reading. Words pass before you—names, things, and places. As soon as you scan another line, the previous is gone. Our outgoing artillery barrages are that way to me. I become that detached. I sit and watch our artillery hit just outside the wire and smoke cigarettes and drink coffee, my demeanor no different than that of someone casually reading the Sunday paper and listening to music.

It takes some incoming to snap me back to reality. Incoming is like the roller coaster at the top, when the clickety-clack stops. As soon as the incoming starts, I know that—like it or not—I am taking the ride the ride's way and not mine. Just hang on is all you can do. Just hold your breath and try to make it through.

Incoming Rockets and Arty

Most of the rockets come from Hill 881 North. Our people on 881 South can see the rockets as they are being launched. After a while everyone at Khe Sanh who can listens in on 881 South's radio frequency. At my company I have a loudspeaker hooked up outside my bunker. If South says "Rockets!" over their radio, my radio operator yells "Rockets!" over the speaker.

In a handful of seconds we can hear the rockets live. Imagine a jet plane on full power coming in and crashing. That's what a rocket sounds like. More than that, a rocket has a grinding scream to it. Fuck the runner's high. You don't get any fucking higher than taking rockets. But when it's all that intense, you don't enjoy it. All you can do is feel it. You can feel your nerve endings sizzling.

I remember one rocket attack. J.B. and I look at each other as though each is waiting to watch the other go. Our eyes blinking, jerking with every hit. I can see everything bouncing—shaking from the explosions. Dust falling from the roof. Two more rockets hit. We each see the terror on the other's face. As the silence and the dust settle, we hear one of the sergeants snoring. J.B. and I start laughing.

I ask that sergeant why incoming doesn't bother him. He says he feels as safe as possible in a bunker. He knows you can get it anywhere in Nam, any time. His fear is booby traps and mines. He'd worked around Da Nang in VC villages doing his first tour. Booby traps, punji sticks, and mines scare the shit out of him. He says that when he was out on patrol there, he shit himself every minute he was out. My way isn't his; his way isn't mine. Most everyone agrees with me versus that sergeant. Most guys tell you that rockets and artillery get their vote. Guys in Khe Sanh, anyway.

Rockets kill with blast power and big chunks of shrapnel. Rockets cut arms, legs, and bodies in half. Just like getting it from the Grim Reaper. From his scythe. Artillery punches big holes in guys.

Between the rounds of arty are the noise and the smell of men in close quarters. Cots, gear, stinky rotten bodies. Radios going. Not music—air group. In the background, bombs going off. Artillery firing. All these impressions cease as soon as artillery starts. When incoming starts it is like that E. F. Hutton commercial. All fucking ears. Am I going to get hit or not? If you are hit in your bunker, you are gone. You know that.

After the bang of a nearby hit, first a hissing sound, the sound of the Coleman lantern that burns JP-4 jet fuel. The blast has knocked the flame clean off the mantel. Then your heart, the sound of your heart pounding in your chest and ears simultaneously. Then you notice the lantern. Relighting. You're alive. The falling dust is casting a haze like a smoggy day in L.A.

All in the blink of an eye—from the time of the bang until you finish the process. That's incoming.

If someone held open the door to a furnace and told me that I could stop the incoming by crawling through, I'd be a burn victim. That's the way I feel. But I don't do anything about my feelings. What is there to do?

Death Report

I get the word that Topsoil has eaten it with six or seven other guys out in a trench line. Topsoil, the kid with the funny laugh and scuzzy head. They were in their bunker when a rocket penetrated but did not detonate. All the men in the bunker ran out into the trench line. The next rocket hit on top of them like a right cross. It knocked them all down like bowling pins.

I ask the adjutant to get me Topsoil's death report. I study it in my bunker. It has drawings of a man on it. Drawings of a man from various angles. Wound will hit you from different angles, death will too. Topsoil's form has the head and half the body marked out. That's it. That's what he's going down in history as, a standardized form with parts marked out.

"How the fuck do you know?" I keep saying over and over as I gaze at his chart. Against a dusty sandbag wall, I sit and think. If he's missing as much as it shows, how the fuck do you people know it's him? You don't know him. You'll never know him.

Reassigned

I am a line commander. My essence as a Marine is to be on the line. I had never thought about or felt or dealt with any other possibility. In late February I am reassigned as the S-2, the intelligence officer.

There really isn't shit to do after a while. As S-2, what the fuck am I supposed to say? "Yes, Colonel, Charlie has been pounding our ass for weeks now. All indications are that he will continue to pound our ass until either the bombing catches up to him or somebody goes out there and makes him stop." There is not much for anyone to do after a while. The only guys with overtime jobs are the guys at medical and graves registration.

I am an advisor to the colonel, to air, to arty. My job is not directly related to personal involvement. It is so much more detached than being a line commander. I now have time to think of myself as separate, an individual in an organization rather than being the organization. I hate it.

I learn about being alone in Nam. The realization creeps up on me like water coming to a slow boil. I fully realize that I am there all alone. We are all doing hard time together, but alone.

Fantasy

I start to have a recurring dream. In the dream I am invisible. I go out alone at night with a packful of bullets and a .22-caliber pistol with a silencer. I make my way silently and invisibly through enemy lines. I do gooks all night—one shot each, in the head, point blank. I cut off their left ears and put them in a sack. I do gooks like that all night long, quietly. I never do everyone in a unit, just some. Charlie would wake up the next morning and see a bunch of his buddies done that way—head shot, left ear gone. If that wouldn't fuck Charlie up, I don't know what would.

I come back in the morning with a packful of ears. Headquarters poges are all into body counts, and I don't like to bullshit. I just toss them the pack and say, "Here, asshole, count 'em yourself."

The dream seems to refresh me. It is the only hope I have. More and more I begin to slip away, to fantasize not of pleasant memories or of going home but of striking back. Like the cartoon of the two vultures sitting in a tree and saying, "Patience my ass, I want to kill something."

Reason is for old folks and young dreamers. Games to be played on quiet summer days. Reason flows, enhanced by a few beers. Khe Sanh is about reality. Not known by the mind, but as pulled out of the mind. Raw. I never doubt reality again. It is too painful ever to doubt.

Despair

Fitz, our adjutant, looks like an old man to me. He must be in his late 20s. He is a lieutenant, a red-headed, freckle-faced Irishman.

It is late at night, and Fitz has some aerial photos. He is good old-fashioned Irish drunk. Eyes bloodshot and on fire with intensity, Fitz talks with a tongue swollen with whiskey.

"Look at this, Spence. Look. What do you see?"

I see the bodies of dead Marines. It is a beautiful NVA trap. The Marine squad that tried to circle from the right went right between two trench lines. I see the lead squad. It is so easy to see it.

"They ate it, Fitz. That's all. All up close."

"No, Spence. Gas. Gas, gas! They're on their backs. Look at all the guys on their backs."

"Fitz, a gunshot will knock you on your back if it hits you in the chest. It can knock you down. Backwards."

"I'm telling you it was gas, Spence."

"Real good," I say, "but I ain't going to report it. They're dead. Leave 'em be."

Gas. It is the way he must fear most. Mine is arty; his is gas. We all have our own worst way. But fear is not an emotion we can deal with emotionally at Khe Sanh. What can we do, get up every morning and scream "Aaagh!"? As time passes fear coalesces with despair. Watching and talking in the night, Fitz and I are two men sharing despair in a smoky corner of a filthy, littered bunker.

Most people do not understand despair. The realization of despair is a very private thing. There comes a point where a man perceives that he is truly lost. Like a person in a maze who has wandered slowly and then with a great sense of adventure, he discovers that he's lost along the hedgerows. The reality of existence comes on as the panic does. The narrowness and exclusiveness of existence becomes more pronounced. The paths are dead ends. You cannot get out. You do not know where you are. You are so totally trapped. You have only the terrifying emotions.

The answer is not to feel. You shut yourself down. To keep your rubber band from snapping, you shut yourself down. You don't think about it, you just do it. You don't say, "Close the door, there's a draft," you just shut the door. You sandbag yourself in. You get inside yourself, and you can look cool as hell doing it. Each man his own private work of art. Each man frozen like a frame in a movie when the projector sticks.

Panic recedes. Quiet despair remains. Cool. Macho.

It is the ultimate macho to look straight down the barrel of death and stick your tongue out at it. To defy that way seals your title, ensures your manhood forever. But you have long since changed your comprehension of manliness. You want to try it the other way, but by now you have sealed all the accesses to yourself. To your soul. You are lost in the darkness, in the dark bunker of yourself.

I am inside now. I can take anything that comes.

Inside Man

Believe it or not the percentage of guys who go out of Khe Sanh as actual bona fide shell-shock cases is quite low. The brass says it is because of the training and the esprit de corps. Marine Corps doesn't have a fucking thing to do with it in my case. I pull the big steel doors down on myself, set the bolts, and shoot them shut. I close myself down emotionally. Like the rat in a trap that chews its own foot off to survive, I do it because I am a survivor.

Other guys do too. You can tell the ones who are inside by looking at them. A guy is talking to you, but his eyes are looking way off into nowhere. The thousand-yard stare, we call it. You have eye contact, but it is like there is no one home inside. He is so far in, you can't see him.

I am with a major one night during a barrage that lasts almost 4 hours. By the light of a Coleman lantern, I see that man shut himself down. We are blinking and jerking with every hit. Then, he just slows down. His jerk becomes a shrug, then stops altogether. His eyes go blank and hollow out. They sink back in the sockets. By the end of that barrage, he is a new man. An inside man. He goes on R&R right after that.

When he comes back we talk about the night of the barrage.

"I lost it, didn't I, Ernie?"

"Fuck no! You found it! It's the only way to make it!"

The Daze

I begin noticing less and less.

I am sitting on my cot one day during an artillery barrage from Co Roc. A work detail that had been reinforcing our bunker roof comes scurrying down into the bunker. They crouch along a concrete wall. I'm on my cot looking at them sitting there with their knees pulled up to their chests. The wall falls in on them. No blast or rush, the wall just falls in from the force of a nearby explosion. Now I am looking out at bright daylight. The Marines are knocked down but not injured. Our bunker wall had saved us. The wall had just fallen over like the final domino between life and death.

I say to no one in particular, "You missed." That's all I have left.

The wall pushing in. Marines falling forward. The memory is slow motion.

Mule

That's the last specific barrage I remember. There is nothing to do. There is nowhere to go. Confined. Down in the smoky haze with no sense of time.

Sandbag's either plastic or burlap. Each with its own smells. Sandbag walls. You sleep against them. They are around you. Over you. As sandbags settle and dry, dust filters out. At first it is like a fine layer of dandruff, and then it gets thicker.

Darkness. It is safer in the dark. Lighted areas are for intruders. What light there is casts long and vibrating shadows. They weave and dance with the darkness. You live on the edge of darkness and journey into the light less and less. There is nothing more to plot, to consult. You are just lying there. Forever.

I pass into eternity. Emotional eternity. No feeling. I shut it down a little too far.

My body goes. I get real tired. I lose my appetite. I can't walk. I can't breathe.

Someone puts me on a mule—a dune buggy with a platform—and I am at Charlie Med. Foggy, misty night. I can't remember being hit. What am I doing here? Am I dreaming?

I'm lying on a stretcher along the wall at the bottom of the stairs. Doc My Friend comes down the stairs after doing emergency surgeries. It's late at night. One Coleman lantern casts a stark light in the far corner. Doc recognizes me and rushes over.

"Spence," he says. He starts feeling me all over, like a guy going over a corpse. He sees I'm not hit. He starts taking my pulse. "What's wrong, Spence?" He's almost begging me to tell him.

An IV pricks my arm, and an oxygen mask settles over my face.

STRIP 'EM AND MOVE 'EM

Tests

I go out on the evacuation helicopter the next morning. I'm flown 30 miles to Dong Ha, our division headquarters. At Dong Ha they have an assembly-line operation set up for processing large numbers of wounded. We are carried from the helicopter to a large shed where sawhorses are placed in twos, row upon row. Our stretchers are placed on the sawhorses.

As soon as I'm placed, men cut all my clothes off with blunt-tipped scissors. Like a lamb being sheared. I had been wearing jungle boots, a sweatshirt, trousers, and wool socks. They cut it all off. Even the boots, they cut my boots off. I look down. They didn't get the nuts. Good!

A doctor hangs over me, looking bewildered. They are used to seeing the problem right away—everybody they see is a fucking hemophiliac. These guys are used to going up and down the aisle deciding who gets done first and by which specialist. They have specialists at Dong Ha. For head wounds, amputations, stomach, everything. But this guy looks at me and doesn't see a specialty. He just waves me away with a jerk of his hand. Like "Fuck this guy." I'm not bleeding.

Naked like a chicken going to an oven, I'm carried on a stretcher, IV going in my arm. I'm put in an air-conditioned ward. In a bed. With sheets. White sheets. I'm freezing. The corpsman in this ward is like a little mouse. A barrage hits. Charlie's artillery from the DMZ (the Demilitarized Zone). Sick as I am, I get my ass out of bed. The corpsman holds my IV bottle, and I'm leaning on him with my arm around his shoulder. He helps me to the bunker. We get down the stairs as another barrage hits. He says, "I bet you're used to this, huh?"

"Never. If I was, I wouldn't have gotten out of bed."

He laughs.

Still in a daze the next day, I am flown 60 miles farther south to Phu Bai. Phu Bai had been rocketed the night before—that's the first thing a corpsman tells me. His eyes are big. One hit and we got another believer. I resign myself to the fact that Charlie will follow my ass with rockets or artillery until I leave. He is not going to give me any slack. He knows what I don't like.

Two rockets had changed all those people at Phu Bai. It looks like what you imagine a war-zone hospital to look like. Navy personnel are busy filling sandbags for the walls. When you see Navy people working, you know there's shit happening.

I am in one of those new Quonset huts that is held up by air. It is black, made of rubber, and supported by fans inside. It is air conditioned.

They stick me everywhere with needles. They tell me I might have malaria. Oh great, I'm thinking. That shit can last for life. You can get relapses of it. For the rest of my life, I'm going to be a semivegetable. Not a whole vegetable—not a fucking hole in me. I can see me in a VA hospital. I'm 80 years old. At the top of my chart in big print it says TYPE OF WOUND: MOSQUITO. Delta 6 macho man, taken out by a pin-head mosquito. I can see me and those old vets, old men sitting around with legs missing. They'd never accept me. "Khe Sanh shit," they'd say, "you was done by a mosquito. Don't bullshit us."

Malaria. I'd heard about guys getting it even if they took the pills—taken every one of them, just as I had. But it's like VD. You always figure it happens to someone else.

I see the corpsmen give a rubdown to a guy with a bad fever. They strip him naked, then put one of those big fans at the foot of his bed. They douse the guy with rubbing alcohol while the blast of the fan is directed on him. The corpsmen keep swabbing him with alcohol to lower his temperature quickly. The Marine is screaming like a guy getting tortured.

I start yelling at the corpsmen. I tell them to let me die, don't ever do that to me. If they ever do that to me, I'll kill them. "I ain't bullshitting," I'm yelling. "I'm a killer. I'll kill any man who tries that on me."

The corpsmen don't even look at me. They are like two guys washing a car. The Marine is strapped down, delirious and screaming. Neither corpsman even gives me a look. They know all Marines are crazy.

The doctor tells me the next day to stop threatening the corpsmen. "They're trying to save you guys," he says.

"If that's the only way, Doc, let my ass go. Tell them to let me pass if that's the only way. Fuck it. I been taking heat for over 2 months. I ain't going out frozen."

Tests. I think they do every one on me. They look down my throat and up my ass, nose, ears—everywhere.

Charlie doesn't do me, but the Navy does. Every fucking day they draw blood. Not this pinprick on the finger bullshit, either. Whole big needlesful from my arm.

"Shit, Doc," I say. "What the fuck are you guys doing with all the blood?"

"Tests," he says.

"No shit. But how much do you guys need? I'm going to die from loss of blood."

"We can't find them."

"Who's them?"

"The little critters," he says. Big freaky eyes behind glasses. The doc is almost blind.

"Well, maybe the cocksuckers don't live in my blood, Doc. Maybe they're in my brain. And you're not sticking a needle in my head to find out, either."

A doctor visits me. He tells me that Doc My Friend got word to him. They're going to get me out. Fly me to Tripler Army Medical Center in Honolulu. "Don't sweat it," he says. "Just give me a little while. I'm working on it." He tells me what a great guy Doc My Friend is, that my friend took a live mortar round out of a guy. That's macho. Ultimate macho. Doc My Friend is a man.

Meanwhile, Back in the World

The Corps sends an officer to notify my family that I am in serious condition and that I have been evacuated. None of this Western Union shit; they hand deliver. My wife isn't home when the officer calls, so he goes over to my mother's house. My mom is across the street visiting with a friend. She sees this Marine coming toward her. A Marine officer.

"Mrs. Spencer?" he says.

Her face drops. Right away he says, "He's OK! He's OK!"

Martin Luther King, Jr. is murdered while I'm hospitalized. A corpsman listening to a radio at the end of the ward says, "Hey, some guy shot Martin Luther King."

Guy sitting up in bed next to me goes, "Good, I'm glad someone finally got that motherfucker!" He has a wild-eyed gleam in his eye.

"Shut your fucking mouth," I say.

He just smiles a fuck-you smile.

They're killing each other back in the world. I'm over here doing Charlie, and they're doing each other back in the world. Riots. Murder. The world has gone berserk. All the violence of the war shown on TV has made the people crazy. People at home see more action than any guy in Vietnam. The people back in the world are like kids who see a pirate movie—coming out of the theater, they're all doing make-believe sword fights. People back home see too much war on TV. They go outside and play war. Killing each other.

Only the suckers doing drugs know what is happening. Their country has gone berserk. Those hippies aren't dumb. They are just shutting themselves down until society gets its shit back together.

I like that picture of the hippie girl putting a flower in the end of the National Guardsman's gun barrel. Dumbfuck look on his face; hippie smiling. Hippies have a look in their eyes. Sad. I walk down one path, the hippies the other. Drug withdrawals might be bad, but not as bad as getting sad eyes without the drugs—not like my way. Some of those hippies stay burned out. I can understand that. If drugs do to them what arty does to me, I can understand.

I do the Lamaze method of shutting down. I am a naturalist who shuts down without the use of drugs. Arty is my midwife saying "Push, shut down" every time a barrage hits. You remember a "birth" like that more, without drugs. The memory lasts longer.

Bodysnatchers

I allow myself to think now—not open up, but think. I believe that I am going home early.

I am hospitalized at Phu Bai for a little more than a week. I notice the Agent Orange. The forests are burned away all around the base. I don't think anything of it. Fuck yes, I want to see Charlie. He is a sneaky motherfucker who is invisible most of the time. As far as I am concerned, they can use nuclear weapons on him. If someone would ask me if I thought we should nuke Charlie at Co Roc and 881 North, I'd say, "Give me the trigger." Nuke is not a bad way to go if you're in the killing zone. With a nuke it's just like "Beam me up, Scotty."

It wouldn't take more than a stiff breeze to beam me anywhere. I weigh less than 130 pounds by now. Boy, I could really do some Halloween numbers; I am a walking skeleton. In my hospital gown the effect is complete.

Those hospital gowns—the type you slip your arms into like a straitjacket and tie in back. They are always short; they never hang much lower than your ass. I think the squids do that deliberately just to check Marines' asses. "Oh, let's just take a little check of the tushie while we're doing your pulse, shall we?" I do not trust the corpsmen near my ass. I've heard lots of stories about them. I ask them to let me wear utilities. "Heavens no, this is a hospital not a jungle," one says to me. Do you know what an asshole I feel like walking in one of those gowns? If my guys could see me, they'd do back flips laughing. They'd whistle and ask if I'd been letting sailors in my ass. I know what my men would say. I'd say it to them if I had the chance. I am just like them.

After a few days I start eating again. Doctor tells me that there are lots of diseases here that are unidentifiable. They call them fevers of undetermined origin. That's what I have. Officially. A fever of undetermined origin. At least now the guys in the VA hospital won't be fucking with me. Now my chart would say TYPE OF WOUND: FEVER OF UNDETERMINED ORIGIN. I'd pencil in a skull and crossbones. Nope, men won't be fucking with you if they are not sure what you have. They might catch it.

I had not taken a shit in a long time. The head is out past the prisoner cage. I see a Marine guarding two wounded NVA. They are on cots with battle dressings on their wounds. They're conscious and passively alert. The Marine sits outside the cage on a stool with an M-16 across his lap.

As I settle down on the shitter, I wonder what happens to the NVA prisoners. You don't hear about how they are interrogated. I know they talk. They sing real quick. They have those guys doing opera. I read those debriefing reports on the prisoners we took at Khe Sanh. None of this name, rank, and serial-number routine. Charlie would tell you the last time he slept with his old lady. He'd tell you all his town gossip. Whatever it is they do to Charlie, it works.

After I shit I check what I've done. All I see is just

one small, green turd. It's bright green, flaky, and almost alive. Like the pod in *Invasion of the Bodysnatchers*. That's what this disease is! I've been snatched, and I'm going to be laying these little green things until I die. Vietnam's revenge for all the Agent Orange, I am turning into a fucking plant! My seeds are these little green turds. I have a nightmare that night. Wake up sweating and shaking, thinking that.

Bravo Again

A corpsman comes sauntering over to my bed. "Your outfit is coming in. Loads of 'em," he says. They lay them out everywhere. In every corridor. Every corner. On stretchers. They are all naked and look like they have been pecked by birds. They are all shrapnel jobs. You can see where they had been covered by their flak jackets—there the skin is clean. Everywhere else there are little pecks, swelling up like bee stings. Not bleeding much. Kisses from Charlie. Marines with such wounds will be back on the line inside of a month.

After Bravo lost all those men in the Doomed Patrol, the other companies shifted men to Bravo. I see two of my men from Delta. One is spaced out. He keeps saying, "And the fuckers just kept dropping those mortars on us." Over and over. Delirious, he keeps repeating it. The other is a young black guy who had just arrived before the siege started. This boy's been eating his Cs, and that blood has no trouble with his digestion. The siege does not fuck with his appetite. He's big and solid. The blast hit him on his right side. I'd say it went off about 9 feet to his right. His jaw on that side looks like acne now, and his right arm is all pocked. Same with his right hip all the way to mid thigh. I light him a smoke and hold it for him while he takes drags. He tells me the story.

Bravo went out under fog, right out the gate at 'em. Hell of a fire fight. Charlie hit back with mortars. Bravo got back all the bodies of the guys from the Doomed Patrol. Paid, too, but Bravo went out and got their guys. Even though the bodies were skeletons by now. Things rot fast in Vietnam.

Ken, Bravo's CO, was wounded, but he would not allow himself to be evacuated. He walked out with his men.

Curtain Call

I am not at all comfortable with what I have allowed myself to become at the hospital. Clean sheets. Hot food. Showers. Air conditioning. Seeing those men from Bravo. They are going back. They got carried out—not with a fever, but with real wounds. And they'd be going back.

The doctor is incredulous when I tell him I feel fine and want to return to my unit. I am released in a few days and travel to Dong Ha to rearm. To get back into Khe Sanh.

I'm going back because I'm not done. My battalion will be going back out; I'm not finished. I've had more than enough, but I'm not finished. I'm a Catholic. I'm a Marine. Macho is a motherfucker.

Doc My Friend is standing on Main Street when I get back to Khe Sanh. I can tell the siege has let up. Marines are moving around. No Sunday strolling, but a lot of open activity. Doc is dumbstruck.

"What happened?" he says. "They told me they would get you out. No problems."

"I needed to come back. Doc, I'm OK."

"No you're not, no you're not. You're a fool." His face is a look of grief and frustration. It is as though I had betrayed him. I had betrayed his friendship by coming back to this place of death.

He isn't me. I'm sorry I hurt him, but he isn't me. Somehow I just feel that it isn't over.

DEATH AS A LIFESTYLE

War's Over

"War's over." That's what my S-2 clerk says when I see him down in the bunker. For several days there's hardly been any incoming.

The battalion bunker has brand-new heavy wooden beams reinforcing the roof. Stateside wood—none of this Vietnam shit. Everything from Vietnam rots fast, even the logs. No matter what time of the year, you put a Vietnam log up for a bunker post or use it for a roof, and termites appear in one day. Termites must be NVA.

I go over to see Ken. He's been hit in the shoulder and he's tired from the recent battle, but he's jacked up. His artillery officer—a nice kid, married—was killed right off. He was calling a fire mission when he ate it, and he held the mike open, frozen in death. You can only transmit or receive on a field radio; you can't do both at one time. He froze out the entire arty radio net.

Ken took a 61mm round right under his armpit. He heard it whistling in and hit. It was a dud. He looked

199

down and saw the fin sticking out of the dirt. That close. As Ken listened to me and my tales of the bush, now I listen to him. He's like a fighter who's telling his fight to an ex fighter who is his friend. He is not bragging. There is no need. We both know what it is like to lose and win. To look down the barrel. He shares the battle because I was not there. Men who were my men went out with him that day. He had avenged his company as I had avenged mine.

The guys coming out of the siege might be inside and all, but they can still pull triggers.

The day after I get back, I'm walking with the S-2 clerk from the trench line back to the battalion bunker. I hear the boom from Co Roc. Not loud—like a far-off echo. I do my Pete Rose stolen-base dash and slide. Now the big booms hit in front—two 152mm.

"War's over, huh?" I say to the S-2 after we get down into the bunker.

"Was till you came back."

Getting Saved by Doggies

Charlie must have said, "Hey, let's watch the U.S. Army embarrass those little fuckers at Khe Sanh." When the doggies get there, everyone else is pulling out. The Marines feel it is just about over. Khe Sanh and everything around it for 6 miles is now a moonscape.

A doggie general drives up outside the base. He has some of his guys trample down some wire, and he positions a film crew inside. Then he starts doing a MacArthur number. Instead of wading ashore, though, this general is coming over the wire. Over and over he films it, mugging for the camera.

Marines are sitting around laughing their asses off. I wonder if that lifer son of a bitch shows that as part of his prize war story? I'll bet that doggie sends that film all over the Army, worldwide. General So-and-so rescues the battered Marines at Khe Sanh.

I love the cocksucker's timing. To think I get my ass out of a clean bed to fly back here to see this.

His men show up in straggling groups—tired little doggies. As if each man carried an axe, they hold their rifle barrels and rest the stocks on their shoulders. If I ever saw one of my Marines do that in the field, I'd have my foot so far up his ass, it would hit his heart. The doggies look like a bunch of woodcutters dragging their asses home from work.

I get saved by 1968's version of MacArthur and his woodcutters?

Valley Sweep—
Reflections on the Shadows of Time and Space

The doggies arrive in force at Khe Sanh. Our battalion is ordered to sweep up the valley floor toward 881 South. It is the first time that our entire battalion has gone out into the field in over 4 months.

With all the casualties we had sustained during the siege, many of our men are new. They have not been out beyond the wire before, ever. Bootcamp to siege. What's more, many of the riflemen had been transferred from support groups so we would have more men in the field.

As we move out through the low ground to the west of the base, a sister battalion is sweeping to our left and is being heavily mortared by Charlie. They are on the same ridgeline that I ran on that night in the rain when J.B. called us back. Time changes everything. As an S-2 intelligence officer, there is not much for me to do but go along for the walk and contemplate such ironies.

The battalion on the ridgeline had lost a reinforced platoon early into the siege. The reinforced platoon had moved out beyond the perimeter to act as an observation post on a small, steep hill. They did not have time to reinforce their position with more than a token amount of wire before they were hit. Back at the base I listened to the fight on my radio.

As I watch the same battalion get hit on the ridgeline, I remember watching them bring the dead Marines into Khe Sanh the day after the observation post was hit. The tent that served as graves registration soon filled up, and the bodies were stacked outside like cordwood. I went over to see the dead Marines. Their faces. Their form—it was as though they had all blended into one mass. Frozen that way, together. Some with their eyes open. Some with their eyes shut. It was the same with their mouths. I had listened to these men the night before. From their radio transmissions, I remembered them.

I remember them now as our sweep passes over the same battleground that they died on. Not more than 2 months have passed, and I have no trouble recognizing their fighting positions.

Charlie attacked the observation post in force on the side of the hill facing away from the platoon's fire support. It was a very small hill—steep and with little room at the top, like a sharp tit. A number of NVA corpses lie rotting nearby. The remains are skeletal, black, and almost leathery. Charlie also left behind large quantities of ammunition, which means that he split with his tail between his legs or that he is dead. I hope it is the latter.

As we move along the valley floor, a UH-34D helicopter is shot down as it tries to land to remove the wounded from the battalion on the ridge. Another helicopter hovering nearby rescues the downed crew. Less than a half mile away, the doggies are sitting around the airstrip eating hot chow and picking their noses. You can be in or out of it so easily. It is all a case of position and timing.

During that first day out, a lieutenant is killed. A grenade on his belt goes off. I walk through the area afterward. Used bandages and battle dressings are scattered everywhere. The ground is still covered with large pools of slowly coagulating blood. I walk by and look, detached. So detached.

The area is also littered with unexploded packet bomblets. Bomblets activate listening devices, which are also dropped from airplanes. The listening devices must be deaf because the packets are powerful enough to take off part of your foot.

We set up that first evening in a large, relatively open area. My scouts and I set up in a bomb crater. The bomb has made the job of digging much easier. My foxhole is small with a blast tunnel dug forward at the base. I lay out my gear in and around my foxhole—it has become a ritual for me. The rifle is to the right front on its left side so I can pick it up easily. The selector switch is set on semi-automatic. The clips of ammo are stacked on the left side of a shelf that I have carved into the front of the foxhole. I place four grenades on the right side of the ledge. To the right of the foxhole I carve a narrow sleeping trench. In this I place my poncho, pack, and blanket. My pack will be my pillow.

It is a clear and starry night. The forward line opens up a couple of times, but the sounds of the night are the only casualties of the wasted gunfire.

The next day arty—our own of course—hits us while we are registering on our afternoon objective. A white phosphorus shell badly wounds several men. This is the new colonel's first operation in command of this battalion. In two days he's lost one lieutenant and several enlisted men—all to friendly fire. Charlie has not thrown a fucking punch.

We set in on a hilltop. From that vantage I watch 881 South being shelled. How strange to watch my favorite home in Vietnam being shelled. I gaze out at the promontory on the western side of the hill and think of how much has changed for me in 8 months—from the time I lost my first man there until today. How salty I have become. A real live veteran. What I had always wanted to be, but somehow the reality and the preconceived images are not the same.

The battalion command post is set up in a series of bomb craters near the top of the hill. The rifle companies are strung around the hill and on the adjoining ridgeline. I have less than 30 feet of visibility in any direction. The perimeter is only 75 feet away. The entire battalion command group is packed into an area much too small. I do not dig a foxhole. Instead I dig a narrow slit-trench, which will serve as both sleeping and fighting quarters. Since I am so close to the front line, there will not be time to change position if we are hit.

I cut a shelf on the outside wall of my trench. I will sleep on my back with my right shoulder facing the

M-79 Grenade Launcher

perimeter. I place my rifle on its right side so I can roll over and grab it with my left hand while pushing myself into firing position. No grenades because we are all so close to one another. My trench is 2 feet deep, shoulder width, and 6-plus feet in length. If I eat it in my trench, all they have to do is bury me. It's just like a ready-made coffin.

I spend most of the time in or near that trench. I even eat my meal sitting in it because my feeling about Charlie is so strong.

I feel like nothing but an observer; my existence, to the battalion, is meaningless. No one asks my opinion, and I do not offer it. I wonder if the drugs they gave while I was in the hospital have changed me. Now only the immediate things can get my attention—things like explosions and fire fights.

The company commander of the sector I am in allows his men to fire M-79 grenade rounds as harassing fire. The rounds go on throughout the night. That is bullshit. I never would have allowed my men to advertise their positions that way.

A heavy fog comes in a few hours after darkness. With rocks holding down the corners, I stretch my poncho over my trench. Inside the trench I lie curled up with my space blanket around me. In my cocoon I am a caterpillar waiting for the next step in the life process. I smoke cigarette after cigarette, not worrying about light discipline because my poncho hides the ember. But it seems as if almost everyone else has a flashlight going. It pisses me off. I had never let my men do that. If we had to read a map, we'd get under a poncho so that no light would show. In this little place a battalion command group is just too big, and this battalion has too many people in it who have spent all their time being poges.

We remain in the same location the next morning while the rifle companies send out patrols. I hear the mortar rounds leave their tubes. Three quick jumps and I do my patented flying fuck from a layout position right into my trench. I hear them scream in and hit. Bang! Bang! After the sounds of the explosions, the screams are almost instantaneous. Then the sounds of a wailing chant from the top of the hill where the two mortar rounds had hit.

"Corpsman! Corpsman! Oh please, dear God, corpsman!"

I lie in my trench looking up at him as he continues screaming. Poor guy has completely lost it. When people yell that way it's because guys are dead. All he is doing is mourning for the men who are already dead. Charlie has finally thrown a punch.

Four guys have eaten it and a half a dozen others are wounded. The seriously wounded are evacuated immediately; the dead wait.

The colonel tells me to take the chopper out with the dead. I'm to get the latest intelligence at regimental headquarters and fly back out the next day with the scheduled resupply. Several of the men who are slightly wounded also wait with me to take the routine medevac. I like that term: slightly wounded. Like the girl who told me she was a semivirgin; she hadn't fucked much.

The landing zone is a narrow section of the ridgeline just below the battalion command post. This is the only spot clear enough to safely land a helicopter. It is very narrow with steep dropoffs on either side. A detail of men brings the bodies down from the top of the hill. They have no place to put the bodies without blocking the landing zone. "Put them there." I point to a spot in and amongst the brush on the hillside. "I don't think they'll mind." They drape the bodies over the bushes that grow and cling to the steep hillside. The bodies are like scarecrows who have fallen over onto the crops. Half in and half out of their ponchos the bodies hang. It had been a foggy morning, so the bodies are wet. Wet so the pale whiteness of death stands out. Their clothes are soaking, the bodies no longer able to provide the heat to dry the cloth.

Twin blades of the CH-46 pop and whack as though clearing the air in its path. I sit on the strip with the wounded. I'm hunched over facing away from the incoming helicopter. The bird is firing its .50-caliber machine guns at the slope on the Laos side of the hill. It approaches, turns, and sets down facing back toward Khe Sanh. A CH-46 helicopter reminds me of a big grasshopper.

The pilot lowers the stern ramp. The grass is waving violently, the engines so loud. The wounded help carry the dead onboard. I wait for the second pair of dead to be loaded. They carry the bodies in the ponchos in the same way that you see people carrying a dolphin out of water. They had slept fitfully in those ponchos; now sleep would be forever.

I notice one of the helicopter gunners. He's overweight and old. He's got a movie camera going. He's filming this. I run up the ramp. Wind is whirling from the rotor blades, the engines roaring. I jump over the dead who are sprawled out on the floor of the helicopter. I'm screaming, "Hey, fucker! Hey, you fuck!" while I try to butt stroke him with my rifle. I point my M-16 right in his face. He is shocked. He's a master sergeant and new incountry. He's wearing clean utilities and is stateside fat.

Marines do not film their own dead. Marines will pose with and film dead NVA all day, but not dead Marines. Not in my Marine Corps, anyway.

The fat gunner glares at me, then he returns to the machine gun. This master sergeant had taken a fun ride as a door gunner to experience the war. He is probably an office poge who is taking pictures to impress the wife and kids. Fucking poge has to create his own image of himself as a hero. It really pisses me off for that fat-ass cocksucker to use dead Marines to play his fantasy out.

As soon as the helicopter takes off, he opens up with the .50 caliber. He just starts spraying the machine gun in a random fashion, like he's trying to impress me or something. The wounded Marines are seated on the jumpseats across from me, their deep eyes searching me for what I might do.

The helicopter shakes as it flies, it vibrates. I notice one of the dead. Face down—what's left of his face. He looks like a pumpkin with most of the meat cut away. He is hollow inside of his head, and the entire top of his skull is gone. His lower jaw is completely torn off. His nose is missing. The right side of his face is all that is left except for one eye, which hangs from the socket. I sit several feet from him, vibrating. Everything's vibrating.

As soon as we land at Khe Sanh, the graves registration guys come onboard. I wait for that sergeant to look back at me. The entire flight back he had been staring out the gun window. I stand in the center of the helicopter. I take my helmet off and cradle it on my left hip just like a football. I stand that way, glaring at him. I want him to take a good look at the guy that almost killed him.

Short Time

After I meet with regiment, I return to what is left of the battalion. The executive officer, a few radio operators, and some supply guys are all there are. Everyone else is out in the field as riflemen. Such units as motor transport no longer exist in my unit.

I report to the battalion executive officer as ordered and to tell the story of the dead and how they died. Telling is our way of remembering—a ritual that had evolved in our battalion. Those who were witnesses told of the dead man's last moments. We were happy for him if his death was quick. (A head shot was best. Boom! Lights out real quick.) We would wish him all the happiness he could have in dying. But as I tell of the lost Marines, I see no feeling in the exec.

The exec is spic-and-span clean. He's got his boots polished, he's clean shaven, and he has brand-new clothes on. They're dark, shiny green. I'm wearing a piss pot, no shirt, an open flak jacket, and filthy trousers. The exec tells me I'm out of uniform.

I say to him, "Major, I just flew down here with a bunch of Marines dressed just like me. I don't give a fuck about your goddamn uniform requirements."

Several enlisted men are present. He calls me a short-timer. He tells me that I've got a short-timer's attitude.

"It's people like you who made me a short-timer, Major."

"Good, I'm glad," he replies.

We are all the fucking way different.

The battalion is called back in the next day. I walk out to the quarry to meet them, and we spend the night out there. I get the word we're going to the beach.

The next morning the entire battalion gets a helicopter lift out. No fucking around and packing. Just get your ass on the grasshoppers and go. Ten months of my life kissed goodbye just like that. All that time up in the mountains. I had become a mountain man. What would I do with civilians? The coast is populated.

John Wayne, My Ass

I take a seat next to the door gunner on the forward jumpseat of a CH-46. Half a rifle platoon has boarded with me.

As soon as we're at cruising altitude, the pilot removes his flight helmet and places it on his lap. Looking back at me he says, "Relax, I'm going to get you out of this." He's got a big John Wayne smile on his face.

I jump to my feet and lunge at him. "Fuck you! Fuck you!" I scream.

I watch that John Wayne smile melt. I'm not sure if he can hear what I'm saying, but I know he is bothered by my snarl. I stare at him until he turns his John Wayne ass around. He puts his helmet on and does not look back.

Wonder Beach

Shallow water and clean sand is Wonder Beach. It serves as an emergency resupply point run by a doggie supply unit. Wonder Beach is a few miles south of Quang Tri City, a sector that has so much going with Charlie that there is no pier large enough for the supply ships. They sit offshore and unload directly onto huge amphibious landing craft. The amphibious tractors drive right up onto the beach to unload. Amphibious tractors driven by doggies. I'll bet that gives a few admirals hemorrhoids.

We left most of our gear at Khe Sanh. We get new clothes and gear at Wonder Beach. We even have showers. Our battalion command post is next to what had been a school built by the French. We do not occupy the building; we build sandbag bunkers around it.

There are all sorts of building materials at Wonder Beach. They have good, new iron landing mats—big steel plates that interlock to form an LZ—and they have new lumber. For the first time we even have real sand for the sandbags—not just hard soil like at Khe Sanh.

Our battalion is assigned to perimeter guard duty.

Our gun positions are far apart because of the size of the base, but the flat land compensates for our thin defense. There are no villages around Wonder Beach—just open, sandy, barren ground.

Vegetation doesn't begin until a quarter mile inland. Farms begin where the soil can support crops. Small fishing villages are to the north and south of us. The village to the south is supposed to be friendly; not so with the villages to the north. Charlie is very tight with just about everyone in the area.

We have five men from the surrounding villages living with us. They are supposedly on the VC death list. The doggies had left them for us. Who had them before the doggies, I'm not sure.

Out of the entire area, there are five people who like the side I'm fighting on? Fuck me.

One of the friendlies claims that he's a captain in the local militia. My NCO in charge of our Kit Carson scouts has all his men salute this alleged ARVN captain with just the middle finger showing. This guy soon figures out what it is about. But you know how Marines are; the more he bitches, the more they do it.

All I see these locals do all day is lie around and eat. If the doggie reports weren't so certain of their value, I would send them packing.

Our first patrols around Wonder Beach are to the south of the base. As indicated by the doggies, the villagers are friendly and cooperative. They report no VC or NVA operating around their villages. Initially, we do not plan to venture north or inland. Helicopters take frequent fire while approaching the base, especially from the north.

Highway 1, the one and only north-south highway, runs inland from the base a few miles. Bernard Fall—the historian who had written about the French defeat in Vietnam, which had happened only 14 years earlier—called the road The Street Without Joy. It's only a two-lane blacktop that would be considered a back road in the world. But after Khe Sanh, it is like a turnpike to me.

The doggies had painted a billboard on the wall of the school facing the ocean, just above our command post. The sign is over 15 feet across. It shows the profile of a black horse with a yellow stripe through it, the ensignia of the Air Cavalry. Supposed to be bad motherfuckers. (I'd be bad too, if I had to lug all that paint around.) Of course the cavalry had long since changed from horses to helicopters. I swear those fuckheads ride to the toilet in a helicopter.

It is at Wonder Beach that I see firsthand how the soldier travels on his "stomach." The ships lying at anchor offshore. Millions and millions of dollars worth of gear. Tons and tons are fed to the war.

One of my scouts is from Louisville, Kentucky. He has met a doggie lieutenant who is also from Louisville. My scout tells me that if I give him one AK-47 gook rifle to give to the doggie, we will be in Fat City. I give my scout the rifle, and we go to a party at the doggie's place.

The doggies have a beach cabana made out of shipping containers. They had cut the walls open and added roofing. Each container is a separate room. They've got a veranda facing the ocean. Nice chairs. Fans, refrigerators, music, cold beer. It knocks me out. Here's some 22-year-old from Kentucky whose whole view of war is a constant beer blast. He can be drunk all day yet get us anything for the price of a gook rifle, so he can go home and tell all his great war stories.

He is lucky, and I have misplaced my sense of irony; I drink beer with them and get good old-fashioned falling-down drunk. I think they barbecue steaks. I can't remember.

At Sea

It is almost a mystical experience, those first few days at Wonder Beach, a near-paradise that reminds me of the beaches in old Hawaii. Mountains to beaches, just like that. To go from the hellhole of Khe Sanh to a beautiful beach. My emotional being is being rocked by the conflict. I wonder at times if I have eaten it and just don't know it.

Most of my men go swimming in the afternoon. I have no desire to relax. Coming back from R&R and from the hospital had been too hard on me—I don't want any more respites. The war is not over. Not for me, it isn't. This place might look like paradise, but it is still a full-time war zone as far as I'm concerned. I just do not let up.

One day the guys try to take Quong, our Bru scout, swimming with them. Quong must be one of the first of his aboriginal tribe to see the ocean. There are slight waves breaking on shore, waves about 2 feet high. Quong freaks. Goes bullshit and runs out. He's gulping like a guppy. He thinks the water is trying to eat him. Man, if he has that kind of paranoia about nature, just imagine what war must do to him.

I had always loved to swim. As a child, playing in the waves was the best thing I could do, and I swam on a team in high school. At Wonder Beach I find that I am afraid of going swimming, and I only go near the water if I have to.

Fear of waking up to a dream possesses me. Perhaps my fear is that while I am swimming, I will realize that I am dead.

Military Intelligence

While walking back with my assistant S-2 from the mess tent after the evening meal, I hear the familiar soft boom followed quickly by a loud explosion. Crack! Then the round comes over us and hits right on the perimeter. I watch the second round hit one of the perimeter bunkers. The arty is coming from the sea!

"No fucking way has Charlie got the goddamn ocean," I yell to the S-2.

Another round goes over us and impacts. We run to the command bunker to find out what is going on. I keep yelling to my lieutenant as we run, "There's no fucking way Charlie's out there!"

Squids. It's the fucking squids. Navy fired three rounds on us. A destroyer offshore and out of sight had hit us with her 5-inch gun. Some bozo fired several miles off target; he was supposed to be firing to the north on suspected enemy positions. And to think I thought just Marine artillery was fucked up.

It is dark. Several Marines had been killed. Corpsmen are working on the wounded before evacuating them to Dong Ha by chopper.

"Go out there and get me that fucker's name." The colonel's eyes are pinwheels as he talks to me. His lips are quivering. "Go out and get me that ship captain's name." He repeats it over and over again.

The colonel gets the doggie base commander to assign one of the Navy patrol boats for Marine duty. I meet the patrol boat and the American and Vietnamese crew at the small pier. The Navy man in charge is an enlisted first-class petty officer. He tries to talk to me and be friendly. I have my standard nasty-ass expression on.

"How many did you guys lose?" he asks.

"We didn't lose a thing, motherfucker," I say. "We found 'em all."

The sea is calm, the swells no more than a foot. As we approach in that tiny patrol boat, the ship seems much larger than I had imagined. The destroyer will not put a ladder down for me to come onboard. I can hear the first-class petty officer radioing and requesting permission. "They've ordered us to back off," he yells to me.

I'm looking up at the bridge of the ship. It is dark. No sailors are standing out in the open, near the railings. I imagine the ship's captain cowering up there on the bridge. It is as though the entire crew is trying to hide from me. Afraid I might see them. The diesel engine of the patrol boat is the only constant sound. The swells gently lift and lower us like a mother rocking her baby very slowly. The destroyer is silent and still. The swells have no effect on the large ship.

I wonder about that destroyer captain. Probably a lifer, shitting himself about his career possibly being ruined. Fuck the dead guys.

I yell up toward the bridge. "You killed Marines, Captain. Put it down in your log. Confirmed kills. No bullshit. You're fucking deadly, Navy. Real killers. We're the 26th Marines. Now do you want to tell me who the fuck you are?"

I write the number of the destroyer down as the patrol boat backs off and heads back toward shore.

Standing there, gazing down at the dark waters passing by, a feeling comes on me. I want to dive in. To dive as deep into the water as I can. I want to swim under water and come out at some other place. Away from this shit. We are killing one another. Friendly fire. Some friends.

My first great intelligence mission, and I had accomplished only part of it. I had a number, but no name. My first intelligence mission, spying on our Navy. Taken there and brought back by the very same Navy. I go to bed late that night, feeling totally bewildered. Just let it be, Ernest. Finito.

Promotion

My promotion to captain finally catches up with me at Wonder Beach. It is only 9 months late. I think it must have come in with all the supplies that now pour in. I wouldn't be surprised if it had been stuck in there with a load of toilet paper.

The colonel insists on a formal ceremony. Ken gives me a set of his captain's bars, and he and the new Delta 6 pin them on me. Mike, the communications officer, and the rest of the guys give me a ration of shit about how they liked me better as the most senior 1st lieutenant in the Marine Corps. Now I'd just be another asshole captain like them. It is a touching ceremony.

I never thought I'd make captain, and I really thought that it had been my own fault. I knew I had rattled a lot of cages everywhere, and I thought I hadn't been promoted for cause.

I never thought I'd make captain, and now I don't care.

Memorial at Wonder Beach

We hold the memorial service in the vacant school-house at Wonder Beach. With most of the schoolhouse roof missing, it is almost like an outdoor ceremony. The building is probably over 30 years old—a monument in itself when you think about it. It is the only thing in the area that is older than a few years. Only the land is constant; everything else is so transitory.

Senior staff sergeants and officers are invited to re-member our dead at Khe Sanh. (I don't know whose idea the limited invitation is.) Some of the invited men do not come. No one questions their absence. Guys are just not ready to start feeling again. They have more time to do.

The service is conducted by the crazy chaplain, the cocoa addict. He didn't come with us when we left Khe Sanh, and I haven't seen him in over a month. I can't believe him now. He's completely changed. He looks so much older. His hair is longer and slicked back, and he's wearing real dark sunglasses. My first thought is that he had started doing drugs. I am wrong.

I thought the chaplain would just do a eulogy and chant a few prayers, and it would be over. Instead, he reads the complete list of our dead. He's talking in a real deep voice. My last memory of this guy is him stealing my cocoa and chattering away like Joe Dork. Now the grief is all over him.

He's taken some heavy emotional hits himself. I see that he has been taking this as personally as the rest of us. He's hidden it so well until now. All inside. Now the grief stands right out on him. Holy shit, I think. Even God can't protect His own guy.

The chaplain reads the names in the order that each

man died. He reads each man's rank and the company he served in. Every time he says the name of one of my men, I jerk. I can't stop myself. I jerk just like I'm taking a hit. Every one of mine hits me. Face after face of the dead burns an impression in my memory. I keep my focus on holding myself together. Cry later, I tell myself. Not now. I have to hang on—I've got more time to do. Don't let go, I keep repeating to myself.

Ken is standing next to me. He and I stand ramrod straight. At attention. Ken has taken more losses than anyone. Every time a Bravo man's name is read, his head jerks like he's been slapped. Tears are streaming down his face.

Ken is more of a man than I am. He lets himself go and comes back. I'm not that sure of myself. By now I've got only a month left to do. I just can't trust myself to let go. At the conclusion of the ceremony, we each go our own way.

I walk away sick to my stomach. I'm so fucking sick of this. No more memorial services. I don't want to feel anymore.

I remember pictures of the doggie memorial services. Boots, rifles inverted, bayonet stuck in the ground and a helmet placed atop the rifle. What the fuck is that supposed to mean? That's not the way I saw or remember my men. I don't need any symbols for my dead. I know who they were. I feel each one as a man. His death was mine. Inside me. That's a memorial. Fuck the symbolism. Men died, not inanimate objects.

How to Know When You're Not Wanted

Every morning we have to provide security for the road-clearing crew on the new dirt road from Wonder Beach to Highway 1. The crew isn't collecting garbage; it is collecting mines out of the road. Folks are mining the motherfucker.

Most of the time, however, they bury plain metal just to screw up the minesweeper. When the road-clearing crew suspects a mine, they place a small charge. By the size of the bang, you know if it is a mine or not.

There was a house next to the dirt road out near Highway 1. A land mine had gone off under a doggie truck near the house. Doggies couldn't find Charlie, so they took it out on the house. They must have used a lot to blow it away. All that is left is the cement floor. Imagine someone blowing up your house. No trial. Your crime? Proximity.

Isolation and Interrogation

I get word that a patrol boat has picked up a fishing boat that sailed into the restricted area in front of the base. Squids report the people aboard as possible VC. I take an armed detail with me down to the beach. As we arrive, the patrol boat is releasing the small wooden boat from tow. There are two men, two young boys, and one woman onboard. The fishing boat is pointed in front and back and is well weathered. It bobs on the waves uncontrollably. I would not have set foot in something so small and rickety.

As we instruct the people to get off the boat, I notice

the smile of fright on their faces. They are half grinning, half pleading in their looks.

"Blindfold them and tell them not to talk," I tell my chief of scouts, who speaks Vietnamese. I follow standard procedure. I also have them searched and tied. It is the beginning of the isolation and interrogation process.

I get the rest of the men to drag the wooden boat far up onto the beach. It looks so ridiculous. A dozen armed men leading a family in black pyjamas, their arms tied behind their backs and multiple sandbag blindfolds over their heads.

We find nothing in the boat except the fishing net. No fish or food.

We are met back at the old schoolhouse by the ARVNs who live on base. As the supposed ARVN captain pulls off the sandbags from the older fisherman, he lets out a cry of delight. Almost a gleeful yell. I guess he recognizes the guy because the next thing I know he is beating the shit out of him. The fisherman still has his hands tied behind his back. They push him down in a chair and really start working over the guy's face. I can see his face swell up right in front of me, all around his eyes, cheeks, and ears. I stand watching. The rest of the family is kept separated in other rooms, but I'm sure that they can hear the blows, the moans. Finally I can't stomach it any longer, and I stop them. The fisherman is moaning and throwing up from the beating.

"Are they VC?" I ask the ARVN.

"Possible. Sympathizers for sure," he answers.

I am not about to watch this cocksucker and his goons beat the entire family. I decide to do it my way. I have every person including the children questioned separately. Even though I understand Vietnamese, I speak only English in front of these people. I go through the interpreters for all questions. The family soon understands that I am the one. The Man. Their destiny. They all tell the same story. The older man is the husband of the woman and the father of the two boys. The other man is his brother. They were out fishing and drifted off course. They are from a small village to the north of us.

We start the second round of interrogation with the oldest man. "Ask him where the NVA are," I say.

As soon as he says he doesn't know, one of the ARVNs starts hitting him in his face.

"Ask him when he last saw the NVA."

As soon as the interpreter finishes, the guy winces. He knows he is going to get his ass kicked again before he even answers.

"Not for a long time," he says. "They do not come to our village. We only fish and stay in our village." There is a soft, almost pleading quality to his words. He sighs as if waiting for another beating to begin.

The S-3 is with me as well as my assistant, a 2nd lieutenant. The lieutenant joined our battalion after the siege had started. He is an ex enlisted man, a nice guy, and probably 10 years older than I am. His nervousness was pronounced even before the siege had a chance to do it to him. I discuss my plan with the S-3 and this lieutenant. We will pretend to execute the older man. I do not discuss my plan with the ARVNs. After gagging the older man, we fire a shot from the S-3's pistol and take the man away and hide him. The family is still separated.

"Tell the ARVNs to bring the younger brother in," I tell my assistant.

The man still has his hands tied behind his back and is blindfolded.

"Don't hit him, and leave him blindfolded," I say.

He is asked matter of factly to tell us where the NVA are. He speaks so quickly that I cannot understand everything he says. The NVA have moved inland away from the coast. He confirms that some of the VC locals have assisted the NVA but insists none are in his village.

The ARVNs seem disappointed when I have the man removed without a beating.

"Bring in the mother and the two kids," I say.

I have the mother and the boys untied and their blindfolds removed. The mother sits on a wooden chair and the children, who are perhaps 6 and 8 years old, squat in the corner across from her. Quiet settles in the barren room. Sunlight from the open roof casts a glare in the faces of the two boys huddled in the corner.

"Bring the younger one here." I point to a spot about 7 feet in front of the mother. I call the ARVN aside and tell him not to hit the boy on the face or body. "Arms or legs only," I tell him. I start the questioning again.

"Where are the NVA," I ask in English. The ARVN asks the woman the same question in Vietnamese.

Her answer is easy to understand: "Cum biet." I don't know.

The ARVN is carrying a walking stick. He starts whipping the child with it. The kid is squatting with his arms wrapped around the outside of his knees. The blows are hitting the outside of his arms and legs.

He is moaning more than crying out. "Oh, oh," he moans. He does not move or raise his hands to ward off the blows. Instead he takes, and moans, and turns his shoulder into the hits. "Please sir, oh, oh," he says in Vietnamese.

The mother is at the edge of her chair. She's wringing

her hands and jerks as each blow lands on her son. She starts sobbing, then stops. As though she has no right to cry since it is her son who is suffering.

These people are so together.

"Ask her again where the NVA are," I order.

"I don't like this!" my lieutenant says.

"Shut up!" I tell him.

The interpreter yells the question to her. "I don't know," she answers. She is half moaning, half pleading in her response. The boy is shaking with fear. His eyes are lit up—huge eyes. The ARVN starts hitting the boy again. My lieutenant grabs the ARVN by the arm, then shoves him across the room.

"Let me see you outside, Lieutenant," I say to him.

As we walk outside the building, he starts. "I got kids. I got kids. I can't stand this bullshit."

"This is their country and their way," I say. "We're probably going to go out there real soon. If I know this Marine Corps, we're going out there. It's my job to find out what the fuck and who the fuck is out there. This whole area is Charlie's. Don't you read your reports? Now you tell me a better way, Lieutenant, and I'll listen. Otherwise, leave."

"I'm sorry, Captain," he says, "but I just can't help it. I got kids."

"And I got a fucking battalion of Marines. What do you want me to do? Just let these people go? Just believe whatever they say?"

He just stands there, looking at the ground.

"Get out. Go back to your quarters."

I leave him and walk back to the room. As I enter, I draw my pistol from my holster. I squat in front of the mother. "Ask her where she thinks the NVA might be." I repeat the question for the interpreter so he understands.

"Inland. I think they went inland," she says.

As she speaks her eyes and mine unite. Hers so distraught. Mine so passive. Panic and fear in hers; I feel a calmness. She begins speaking without further prompting.

"They are not in our village." Half the time she is crying and sobbing, and the rest of the time she repeats over again that the NVA are not near her village.

"I think that's all they know," I say to the S-3.

"What do you think we should do with them?" he asks.

"Let 'em go."

Darkness is only an hour away by now. I have the rest of the family untied and their blindfolds removed. The other members wail with emotion as they discover that the father had not been killed as they had thought. I dismiss the ARVNs and am all alone with the family. I speak to them in Vietnamese. I ask the father if he would like to leave now or wait until morning. He says politely that no, they do not want to wait until morning. They ask if they can have their boat back. I tell them that I will have to get a clearance for their boat, but I promise that it will be kept safely for them. I have one of my men get a case of C rations. We give each of them a sandbag full of Cs. Just like Halloween goodies in bags—the bags that had been their blindfolds. They each thank me and bow that jerking submissive bow of theirs before leaving. I walk with them to the edge of the base near the water's edge.

Just another day in their lives, probably. I watch them walk up the beach until they disappear into the darkening horizon. I sit there on the beach well into the night, watching and listening to the waves crashing, rolling, pounding on the shore. The waves keep coming, over and over again. How long have the waves been, I wonder. Again and again they come. Sometimes soft and rushing up on the sand toward me, sometimes with a crash and splash—but endless. I think about endlessness.

I draw my knees up to my chest and wrap my arms around the outside of my knees. My left hand grabs my right wrist. I'm locked in thought. Not even bothering to smoke a cigarette. Brooding, everything churning. All my dreams and desires and aspirations flash before me. My aspirations, my history, my destiny. It was my destiny to have been here today. It all came together for me. I had not only witnessed war; I had orchestrated and conducted it. That day I had achieved my finest work, my greatest accomplishment.

What else is there, Ernest? What further heights will you seek? What will you not do, Ernest? What will you not do?

I go over and over what has just happened. I wonder what is the power of my mind to conceive of such things. How quick I am to seize an opportunity. How utterly brilliant I am. With my boots I dig little trenches in the sand.

The waves grow softer as the evening continues. Soft boom and rush. The waves now race farther up the beach with the incoming tide. The wind is blowing ashore. The mist from the waves leaves salty droplets on my face and glasses. All is in rhythm around me but, inside me, everything is in turmoil.

My reason. It is my power of reason. I am so right. I do things so intelligently. That's it. I am so disgustingly rational. I am so fair. But who am I to decide what is fair, what is good or bad? There is no good or bad when you deal with violence. Not even degrees of good or bad. It's bullshit to say to myself that I could have been worse. I would have done what I felt I had to do to get what I wanted. Only my cunning allowed me the luxury of not having to go further. I stopped because I was sure that they had told me the truth—not just because I wanted to stop. I had used my imagination to get those people to use theirs. I murdered and tortured their minds. I made them torture themselves.

During the interrogation it was as though one side of me watched while the other side did it. On that beach both sides came together again. Yes, I had done it. What made it worse was that it was just like me. I had no trouble identifying my handiwork.

Later that night, after my return to the battalion area, the lieutenant comes to see me. He tells me he is sorry, that he was wrong. I tell him that he should not be sorry. "You're still a human being, I'm a fucking war criminal," I say. "I should be shot for what I did."

I fill out my report. My recommendation is that we concentrate our search for Charlie inland.

Reaction Force

A few days later our battalion goes out on a sweep toward Highway 1. It is the same area where the doggies got hit about a month earlier. No contact, only booby traps. No Charlie.

The day after our operation, the doggies get hit on Highway 1 just before dawn. They are north of the base and inland. A sigh of relief goes through me at the news.

The position of the NVA justifies my actions with the Vietnamese family. I realize that American men have died and feel ashamed of my thoughts. Men are dying, but I was right. I told them so, and I am so smug. How petty and selfish I am. Self-justification. To be so self-centered disgusts me.

I see a pattern in myself: I always place more importance on my involvement in a situation than on the situation itself. My way sickens me. I want to be free. In the past I had wanted to run every show, and I resented being sidelined. Now, as much as possible, I want to finish my tour as an observer. A short-timer.

The battalion organizes a reaction force. I am put in command of the column of relief trucks that will go out with the supplies to the doggie units that have been hit. We take the usual—food and ammo.

It is early morning, and the road has not yet been swept for mines. We are ordered to run the road without waiting for it to be cleared by the sweep team. In my piss pot but without a flak jacket, I ride the lead truck. I carry only a pistol—the first time I go out without carrying real heat, like a rifle. Also for the first time I wear the insignia of my rank. Silver captain's bars on my collars. I sit on the left front fender, feet on the front bumper. I grin my ass off. Joking with the driver, I tell him that I'll watch for the mines. He's going over 20 miles an hour, and I'm going to see mines? I am suicidal.

We get to the first doggie camp in less than 20 minutes. It had been mortared the night before. I can still see artillery explosions going off beyond the perimeter. The sound of gunfire can be heard off in the distant tree line.

A platoon of doggies is assigned to the convoy as

replacements for the forward units. The platoon commander is a young southern boy still in shock from the shelling the night before. His conversation is almost slurred—he half talks, half mumbles. I think to myself, son, how are you going to make a full tour?

We drive up a narrow dirt road from that first camp to the forward units that are still going at it with Charlie. By now I am standing on the side fender next to the lead driver. The doggie lieutenant stands on the seat of the truck next to the driver. The truck windshield is down, and it has sandbags piled on the fenders for blast protection. A .50-caliber machine gun on a turret is just behind the driver's seat. As we approach the forward lines, a squad of doggies walking toward the rear approaches. A couple of the soldiers are guarding an NVA prisoner. He is very white looking and completely naked. He isn't blindfolded, but his arms are tied behind his back. The guy looks as if he has all the trouble he needs. That gook is the most humble man I've ever seen. I don't know what the doggies had done to him, but by now he is not a fierce-looking killer at all. The doggie lieutenant in the truck with me yells, "Stop this truck. I'm going to kill that bastard! I want to kill him."

"You keep driving," I say to the driver. "Kill the motherfucker on your own convoy, Lieutenant. This convoy's mine. Just hang on awhile, and you'll get all you want."

"I lost some of my men this morning, Captain. The sneaky bastards hit us with mortars. We didn't even see them." He's about ready to start crying.

"Welcome to Vietnam."

A Hot Breakfast

We drop the convoy at what appears to be the forward command headquarters. The S-3 drives out to meet me. He has a jeep and a driver and one guy riding shotgun. The colonel has sent him out to the various doggie units to coordinate. The thought of doing a joint operation with the doggies sends chills through me. I'm sorry, but I just do not trust doggies.

We drive back down to Highway 1, then head north. S-3 tells me that NVA had hit in several locations with mortars, RPGs, and small arms. Most of the attacks were hit and run, and they lasted less than 30 minutes. A doggie armored unit had been hit just below Quang Tri City, and that's where we're going.

The armored unit is just off the highway, at a bend in the road. Tanks, armored personnel carriers, and other vehicles are all over the place. The vehicles are in a circle. It looks like a wagon-train scene. These boys just can't get out of the cavalry days, can they?

All the doggies look so clean. They're wearing new green utilities, and the vehicles are all new, clean green. Only where a tank took a hit is there anything but new green. The hits are bright silver—metallic splashes on the green surface.

We are supposed to meet with the doggie battalion commander. Since he's still busy trying to sort things out, we get a tour of the camp from a doggie master sergeant.

"How long have you guys been here?" I ask.

"Five days."

Both the S-3 and I look at each other. We both have an I-don't-believe-these-guys look on our faces. There is no wire. Not a speck of wire anywhere. There are no trenches or fighting holes. Nothing.

"Where do you guys stand your watches?" I ask.

"On the tracks."

Any motherfucker stupid enough to sit out in the open like that for a week is an idiot. Marines would have had barbed wire strung and trenches everywhere. When Marines aren't moving, they are either digging or laying wire.

When we finally get to see the doggie colonel, he's still ranting and raving. He's saying how he's going to clean out all the villes in the area. He tells us that the beach is our area and that he was attacked from the east. Since the ocean is east of him, he's implying that it's our fault. This grits-eating redneck sits on his iron ass for almost a week in the same spot with no defenses, and he's trying to tell us we're fucked up?

Believe it or not, they had one of the armored vehicles rigged like a kitchen. Charlie hit with mortars, handheld rockets, and rifle fire when everyone had gathered for morning chow. Charlie had crawled right up on them at night and hit them at breakfast. A hot breakfast, you bet. All that new iron gear didn't do them shit.

"Looks like the fishermen were right," the major says as we're riding back to our base.

"Bet you soon enough we're going to be bopping north of Wonder Beach," I say. "Those fucks will cry the blues all the way to Saigon."

I can just see them telling everyone about how we sit on the beach while they do all the fighting. Those doggies got hit sitting. What did they expect? Charlie hit them because they were where Charlie was, and they gave Charlie the opportunity. Charlie doesn't give a fuck which American ass he kills.

The Locals

I don't know how, but those fishermen I interrogated got whatever bullshit passes they had to get. Vietnam has no effective government, but they still have bureaucrats.

Just the two brothers come for the boat. They are permitted through the front gate only, which was miles from their home. I have my men help them drag their boat into the water. They both smile and thank us for helping them. Some help. We kick the shit out of these people so they tell us where Charlie is, and it doesn't do a bit of good. Who read my report anyway? All those fat fuckers in Saigon who could give a shit less. Those Saigon poges have the best time of anyone. Booze, women, good food. Fuck 'em.

I stand and watch the two men in the small boat make their way through the waves. They hoist a sail that is not much bigger than a bedsheet. The waves pitch them upward and out to sea.

A few days after the doggies took it in their armored kitchen, we are moved outside the base at Wonder Beach. Our battalion sets up along a canal between the base and Highway 1. There is a bridge and villes all around us. Fields from the villes grow right up to our position. The locals walk through our camp all day long. We are astride the road; we cannot control them. Old women and kids try to hustle us and sell us food, baskets, anything. I am so glad that I did not have to put up with civilians for the full year. It's so much easier when you can just drill whatever moves.

They hit us from the villes with mortars—61mm mortars. Just a round at a time, every day or so. I can hear the rounds leave the tube. Thunk! "Incoming!" I yell and run for a bunker. All the VC succeed in doing is to piss us off and mess us up even more than we already are.

Those little shits who walk through our camp are the same ones who plant the mines and fire the mortars at us. Most of the villagers who are smiling and scratching ass with us are VC.

It takes some balls to play the game those locals play. Try imagining yourself and your family doing that for over 20 years—pretending with the foreigners while trying to kill them. I'd never last in a guerilla war. I'd show my feelings—I always wear my feelings up front. I'd never make it. Enemy would take one walk through my ville and shoot me first. Just from the way I looked. I could not pretend.

Then again, I see only the survivors. The locals have had the advantage of 20 years to get rid of all the easy ones like me. Survivors adjust. All the cocky guys like me would be dead. I am fighting the survivors. Survivors are a motherfucker.

I don't buy the line about duplicity and cruelty being a part of the Asian's nature. Anyone in that situation would be cruel. Just try doing their game for a few generations—you'd adjust too. Race doesn't have a thing to do with it. Terror is the most effective tool they have, and they use it. They have no place to go. No other options. So they use what works best for them. They scare the living shit out of us.

I do not like being with the locals. Which one would be my murderer? How could I tell? I try to see, but I never know.

While living with these civilians, I realize I am seeing in a different way. Images of life around me just run through my mind. My focus is on the realization of what I have become—the fruits of my own labor seen in the light of my disappointment and my self-anger. I am a warrior. What does that mean? It means that I am a fool.

Society not only justifies my idiocy, society sanctifies it. "Onward Christian soldiers, marching as to war. . . ." There isn't a Christian thing about war. If Jesus is supposed to be about love, then there is no way that he'd have a thing to do with war or violence. Jesus wouldn't. Not the Jesus I knew.

ARVN Operation

The ARVNs drive up in trucks at our forward base along the canal outside Wonder Beach. I am assigned as the liaison officer to this ARVN operation, a sweep up the coast and inland through the farms. The worst VC country in the area. I take a detachment of a half dozen Marines: scouts, artillery, and radio operators. As the only Marine officer, I will call in air strikes and air evacs. If these ARVNs get hit or hit Charlie, I'll call in whatever they need.

The ARVN battalion commander is a captain. Young-looking guy. They have a doggie advisor who is also a captain, and there is also an Australian warrant officer with this unit. These ARVN troops look like the most battle-hardened suckers you can ever imagine. Skinny little fuckers, they look like a bunch of weasels coming off those trucks. There are fewer than four hundred of them—a battalion is supposed to have 1,100 men.

Another "battalion" unloads on the other side of the canal. We will be operating abreast of this group. Villes line the canal. Dikes, paddies, fields, and tree lines—the map shows square after square of them—is what we will sweep through all the way to Quang Tri City, 5 miles away.

All my guys are wearing flak jackets and carrying full battle gear. I wear a piss pot but no flak jacket. I notice that the doggie and the ARVN captain are only carrying pistols, so that's what I carry. I can still play Marine Corps macho. Maybe I'm still suicidal.

I walk at the front of the Marine group beside the Aussie. As we pass through our wire, the ARVNs break up into small units and fan out over the fields. They scatter quickly in a half-trot type of run. The paddies are dry and nearing harvest. The seeds are brown on stiff, short stalks. The radio operator carrying the radio to my battalion gets so scared that he starts throwing up. The senior NCO, a corporal E-4, takes the man's radio, kicks him hard in his ass, and tells him to go home. "Get the fuck outta here, sweetheart!" We are only 450 yards out.

All my Nam training centered on operating in villages. For over a month at Camp Pendleton in California, we practiced going through and attacking villes. Here it is close to a year, and this is the first time I do it for real. But it doesn't seem real. I feel as if I am on some weird safari. The ARVN soldiers zigzagging like beaters or hounds or hunting weasels, driving the game forward. I walk along the central path that follows the canal. Punji traps are everywhere. Real ones—not like school. Fortified ville after fortified ville. Hedgerows, punji traps, booby traps, and fighting holes. Each ville just a few huts with thatched roofs, homes with dirt floors. No men, not even boys. Only women and children in the villes. But someone is knocking these women up.

They move very quickly, these ARVNs. The Aussie

tells me that the ARVN battalion commander is the best one in the entire division. He is very aggressive. His style is to get right into it—no bullshit, just jump right in.

My Bru scouts are nervous out here with the ARVNs. They do not like ARVNs, and they do not like villes. They are mountain boys.

We stand out like sore thumbs. The ARVNs wear form-fitting clothes. We Marines look raggedy. Most of us still have our Khe Sanh piss pots and flak jackets with the reddish tint. Those ARVNs must think that we are part of a circus troop.

The battalion on our left is having trouble keeping up with us. We stop continually to wait for them to catch up. I sit on my piss pot, watching the other battalion trying to move abreast of us. In a hedgerow the men hit a trip wire and set off a booby trap. Three guys get taken out by an 82mm mortar round. The doggie captain with us laughs. "They're always doing that in that battalion," he says. The Aussie tells me that the other battalion is useless. He smiles at my look of bewilderment at their callousness.

We make contact just before noon. The ARVNs really let go. They are all firing on full automatic. The ARVN battalion commander just keeps walking casually toward the fighting going on 300 yards inland from the canal. The doggie captain and the Aussie follow him. I can see my guys spreading out. They fan out just like they're expecting to do their own thing at any moment. Turning side to side, rifles hip high, pointing as they turn.

I tell my NCO who carries the battalion radio and the arty radio operator to follow me. "You other guys stay here," I tell them. I get no arguments. They all just go down into fighting positions, covering each other.

I walk beside the Aussie, asshole that I am. We're

playing macho. He's walking casual, so I walk casual. I'm not letting these suckers put down the Marines. Fact is, though, that Marines do not play these kind of games. If shit is going on, Marines do not tempt fate by walking out in the open. My training tells me to go into the half crouch and move in short bursts, dropping between runs. If you have to move toward firing, that is how you should move. These guys are doing a Sunday stroll.

"It's just a little thing," the ARVN CO yells over to me. Like he's talking about some guy's dick size.

My battalion had been asking for a report since we reported contact.

"My battalion would like to know if you need anything," I say to the ARVN. I'm like a bartender or something.

"Oh no, no, no. This is nothing at all. Just a few VC," he says.

The firing soon dies down, and we return to the canal. The battalion command group has several flunkies who serve the officers. The flunkies start cooking fires. They cook rice in a piss pot. The ARVN captain invites me to dine with him. The captain, the doggie, the Aussie, and I sit down to eat on a tablecloth spread out over the ground under a tree next to the canal. A flunkie gives me a porcelain rice bowl and chopsticks made of ivory. Bowls of different entrees are placed in front of us. Besides dishing out my rice, one of the flunkies asks me if he can make me a cup of coffee or tea.

"How about milk?" I say.

He looks bewildered. The doggie captain laughs. All the dishes except the rice are C rations. Ham fried. Beef spiced with sauce. Beans and franks. Hamburger and beans. I sit on my piss pot. The Aussie sits on his ass, while the doggie and ARVN captain hunker gook style. They say a good hunker—a tight hunker—is when your balls can just touch the ground. Not the ass, just the balls.

The doggie captain starts in with his war stories. Tells me how great this ARVN captain is—how brave he is and how much his men admire him. The ARVN captain starts complimenting the doggie. He tells me how brave the doggie is. They both tell of the time the two of them got wounded by shrapnel. Each tried to get the other to get on the medevac, but they both stayed. They had a definite academy-award act going. I would not have been surprised if they had started sucking each other's dick. I just keep shoveling food in my face. Just me and the Aussie are chowing down; the other two hardly eat. They just want to talk about war.

"How long have you been incountry?" the doggie asks me.

"Year," I answer.

"Where have you been?" asks the doggie.

"Khe Sanh."

"Ohhh." End of conversation. No further discussion of war.

As the doggie is insatiable in his appetite for the war, more and more I find myself reaching, grasping for peace. In almost any situation my inner self cries out for it. At any time, in any setting, my eyes seek out only the beauty. As the doggie told of battles, my mind's eye focused on a sumptuous meal elegantly served beside a canal. I hear only the sounds of the stillness of midday, the sounds of gunfire and grenades a forgotten memory. A life past. For a moment I drift inward, taking with me the pleasantness of a full belly and a cigarette. I rest there—far, far away from the hell I walk in.

As we get underway, I notice two girls being led to the canal by several ARVNs. The girls are in their mid to late teens.

"You might want to take your men up ahead," the Aussie says to me.

"Yeah, OK." I tell my NCO, "Let's go. Get the guys and let's go."

"Are they going to fuck 'em?" he asks me. We are walking along together, and he asks me again, "Skip, are those guys going to fuck 'em? Are they going to gang bang 'em, huh?"

"I don't think so."

"Well what the fuck are they going to do?" he asks.

"Teach 'em to swim, swim under water, you know? See how long they can hold their breath."

"Oh, water torture!" he says.

"You should stay in intelligence. I think you got a good shot at a career."

"Why them?" he asks.

"How do I know, maybe they just like doing young pussy. We just stepped in it, and I guess they want to know if we're going to be seeing any more shit this afternoon. You notice that these guys didn't fuck with any people until we got hit. I guess those two girls were the nearest to where it happened. You remember earlier, when the ARVN lieutenant beat the shit out of his own man who tried to steal the chicken? This is a tight unit. These ARVNs know what they're doing. They're not reckless."

A while later the Aussie joins up with me. "The young ladies agreed with your fishermen friends. All we hit were a couple of local VC. They say that the NVA units are inland. Looks like they'll be fighting your U.S. Army," he says.

"Ain't my fucking Army," I say.

The Aussie lets out a loud, sarcastic laugh. That was the only time I had heard him laugh.

The rest of the operation is a leisurely walk to the outskirts of Quang Tri City. I ride a jeep back with the Aussie to his barracks.

It is a typical old French building. I think only the French used concrete in their buildings. We are right smack in the middle of the city. Wire and sandbagged guard posts surround the building, but someone could still sneak right up to it—there are houses and other buildings all around the barracks.

"You sleep here?" I ask the Aussie.

"Why?" the Aussie asks.

"I mean you fight the cocksuckers all day, then you just sleep amongst them at night? This is too close for me."

"You're a might suspicious aren't you?"

"I'm fucking alive, Jack!"

We have a few beers in his room, then we go over to meet the doggie captain at an officers' club. The ARVN officers are there. The last thing I clearly remember about the night is the ARVN captain telling me about a battle that had taken place that day. It was just north of Dong Ha. One of his former company commanders is missing in action, killed surely. He keeps going on and on about what a brave and good officer this man was. The most decorated officer in the division, the dead man's name was Lieutenant Mau.

"I am so sad," the ARVN captain keeps saying. "He was like a little brother to me." The captain sighs. The tone and words are touching, but his eyes are passive. Although he had just heard the news moments earlier, it seems as if he is remembering an event and a person long past. His memories for the man had formed and were put behind him so quickly.

Maybe people learn to grieve differently when faced with death as a lifestyle. I slip quietly into a drunken stupor. The clear passive eyes of the ARVN captain are the closing shot of the picture show that I had been to that day. My very own picture show, filmed just for me that day, by me.

Pointless Ceremonies

I had planned to spend the night with the Aussie, but I must have told him that I wanted to be with my men because that's where I end up.

My scouts and men are staying with an American civilian. Is he AID? CIA? Who knows? He works with the Bru. This place has regular house trailers. Stateside, air-conditioned house trailers. All of the guys except the Bru are crazy drunk. Back from a great time at the whorehouse in town, the Marines had torn the place apart. We lie on the floor of the house trailer, battle gear all over the place. It looks like a scene out of my college days when we'd party all night. Guys passed out all over the place. It looks like a massacre. The only difference between college and now is the gear; the rifles and combat gear remind me that I'm not on just another college drunk.

My body always pays for those drunks. My first sense of reality after such times is the feeling that someone has really fucked with me. That someone has beaten me severely on my head and shit in my mouth before they left. That's what I feel when I first open my eyes and try to raise my head—even before I go through the where-the-fuck-am-I routine.

It is a slow-motion morning and a pain getting the guys going. They do not want to go back. They are drinking beer for breakfast. I never could do that; drink first thing in the morning after a heavy drunk.

There is a helicopter pad nearby where we can catch a flight back to Wonder Beach. It is just an open area right on the outskirts of town. Soon after we arrive, the guys wander off. They say they'll return at the sound of the chopper. I wait alone at the landing zone, smoking cigarettes and killing time.

That's what I am doing when I notice all the street urchins. Little boys from 5 to 10 years old all over the place. I notice that one of them has sores all over his legs. I call him over in Vietnamese.

I carry a Merthialate bottle in my first-aid pouch. Some women will not go out without their makeup kit; I never feel complete without my first-aid kit. Mine is a different form of vanity.

As soon as I start treating the kid's sores, other kids swarm all around me. Like pigeons in a park—feed one and you get the whole flock. It seems as though every kid has sores. I notice some of the kids scratching off the scabs so I will give them the treatment too. I use up the whole bottle before treating very many of them. As soon as I run out, they disappear, just like pigeons when the food is gone.

Into and out of my life they go. Our common bond a bottle of medicine. An ointment dabbed like the oils of confirmation. I am like a traveling bishop doing another pointless ceremony.

A Huey comes in. My men come running back. They're great guys. Crazy as hell, but great.

Briefing

Helicopter rides are a dime a dozen to me after a while. I fly back and forth to the regimental headquarters in Dong Ha for intelligence briefings so many times that the trips become a blur, my memories lost to the insignificance of it.

Most of the regimental staff is new incountry and has never been in combat. In one briefing the S-3 has visual aids. To show the various kill ratios and to stress the effectiveness of night ambushes along the abandoned railroad tracks, the guy is using maps and graphs. This clown has filled in the graphs with colored pencils.

I ask only one question, which brings down the house: "Major, what's the ratio of circumcised to uncircumcised NVA in ambush versus straight search and destroy?"

The Last One

The battalion is going north of Dong Ha through Leatherneck Square. Leatherneck Square is a place where you can always count on getting into it with Charlie. Marines and doggies and ARVNs visit the place, but Charlie lives there.

Almost the whole battalion goes out. Crazy Doc is with us, even Fitz the adjutant. Who isn't? The exec.

We ride trucks to Dong Ha from Wonder Beach. We have to steal some of the vehicles from the doggies—they wouldn't give us a ride. We park the stolen trucks outside Dong Ha near the bridge. The other side is a short walk across the concrete span.

As soon as we start across, civilians from north of the base start pouring across the bridge in the opposite direction. You can see the panic on their faces and in their eyes. Everyone is carrying whatever belongings they can. They come across the bridge using that semirunning, shuffling trot. Talk about knowing what you're in for ahead of time.

Ken pulls my chain. "Hey, Spence, what do you think?" he asks.

"About what?"

"About these civilians."

"That's why you're not in intelligence," I answer.

We grin. We both know we are going into it. I can smell Charlie all over the place. Ken can, too. The battalion can. Talk about dogs on a hunt—we are all up. We are grinning and joking about it. That's another Marine tradition, joking around when you're going into battle. I do it because I don't want to lay any of my shit off on others. If I can make others laugh, I will. Who wants a sour puss when you're walking in and you know someone's not going to walk out? I get real serious as soon as I cross that bridge, though. Yep, my asshole jerks about two notches tighter. I am a salty old veteran, but my asshole is still young.

Nothing happens the first day, and we set in early— well before sundown. Our battalion CP is in a small, recently deserted ville with a trench line dug completely around a handful of thatched huts. The trench line makes the ville seem like an island—an island in the sea of war. It was as though the ville had tried to isolate itself somewhat from the war going on around it. I am amazed at how compacted the earth is on this island. The feet of the peasants have compacted the ground until it is like a smooth layer of concrete. There is not a cinder or pebble in sight.

I must stoop to clear the doorway of one home, a home that consists of one room with a bunker in the corner. The bunker has been dug through the wall and down like a cellar, but not a cellar with wine or a pool table. The war is such a part of the peasants' lives that a bunker dominates their home. The hut is very clean and almost elegant in its simplicity. The dignity of these people to keep their homes so clean in the midst of war. I am just a passing visitor. Uninvited and unwelcome.

I see what appears to be a low wicker table. On closer inspection I discover that it is a bed. There is no other furniture. It had become a fantasy of mine to sleep with dignity. I take the bed outside, treating it with great gentleness. I place it next to the trench line. I lay all my gear except my rifle on the opposite side of the trench and try the bed. It does not work; the bed is too short. So much for fantasies. I return the bed to the house. I sleep beside the trench on the ground.

The next day we zigzag beside Highway 1 toward the DMZ. A battalion on the move is stop and go—more stop than go. I sit on my piss pot whenever we stop. The rice in the paddies is dry now; it is ripe and ready for harvest. The stalks of the rice plants are about 2 feet high and turning a greenish brown. The husks on the grains of rice are like a shell. I strip the grains of rice from a single stalk. It is not white and polished. It is more like wheat—brown.

I have casually wasted several mouthfuls of food for someone. The farmers lose again. Trails veer off in all directions through this sea of grain. It is trampled down by the Marines who cross the field. Hours of work by the peasants—wasted. Their saviors have trampled their future into the ground. I feel somehow that all the peasants want is this rice. Not me, not Charlie; they just want to be left alone.

At the end of that day we find the remains of ARVNs. These are the missing that the ARVN captain told me about that night at the bar in Quang Tri City. I swear that I know the dead.

I see the body of the man the captain had called his little brother, Lieutenant Mau. Wearing officer's insignia, he is laid out on his back alongside the old narrow-gauge rail tracks. He is bloated and turning black. The skin on his face is like the blackened, cracking leather on an old football. His eyes are scaled over with death. Only the flies chant in his memory, their buzzing the repetitious ritual of tiny monks tending to the endless cycle of death and life. The flies protest fiercely as the body is picked up and placed aboard a two-wheeled cart. They hover close by.

I walk the battle scene, analyzing the ambush that Charlie used. It was a classic. Charlie used the raised railway as a reverse slope. The ARVNs had to get very close before they could see or shoot. Charlie took, too. There are no NVA bodies, but NVA bandages with dried blood are scattered all about. Soon after we secure the area, ARVNs come out in trucks to pick up the bodies. Who loads the trucks? The peasants. The bodies, bloated and popping, are hefted aboard. Again the peasants pay the price of proximity.

In some brush near the ville we find NVA packs. I believe they are the packs of the NVA killed in the ambush of the ARVNs. All a man's worldly belongings in his pack. I take his hammock. I also see rice, canned milk, ammunition, cooking gear, and a packet of letters wrapped in plastic from our discarded C-ration boxes. Who delivered his mail to him? How many weeks or months had it taken to receive a letter from home? His life, unknown by me and viewed only after his passing. Will I be viewed in such a way? My ending an idle moment for others?

Fitz leaves the field after a few days. Before departing he comes to see me. "Please, Spence, take my rifle. I think you'll need it."

I take his M-16 and ammo belt. I accept the concern of a friend. Even Fitz the adjutant, the office poge, can smell it. Charlie has his own smell. He is all around us.

We spend the night in the ville where we found the ARVNs and resume the sweep early the next morning. Flat land with tree lines box in the villes. Between the villes are wide open fields—some as large as a half click. All the villes are deserted. Recently so.

We are doing prep fires with arty on a tree line. Short rounds and Marines are wounded in the lead platoon. Fuck arty. Medevac helicopters again.

We bring our tanks forward to prep a ville we suspect is occupied by Charlie. The homes out here have been hit by fire so many times that some are only tattered shells. The fighting holes and trenches scattered in and around each ville indicate battle after battle—some only planned, others fought. We move toward a tree-lined ville. A low ridge no more than 10 feet high runs behind the homes. We move through the open fields, a full Marine battalion on line. Three rifle companies forward and one in reserve.

Chi Com 130mm Cannon

Halfway across the field Charlie opens up on us. Two 130mm artillery rounds. I hear them cough in across my front and Boom! Gray flowers bloom. Instant sweat job on my brow and back. A bombed-out house a hundred yards away is my nearest shelter. The soft soil makes my run a slow-motion event. I keep expecting Charlie to bracket us or come right across us. Before I reach the house I hear our arty from Dong Ha going over us toward the DMZ. By now we have counter-artillery radar. When Charlie fires his cannon, we can fix his position. As soon as I reach what is left of the house, I try to find its bunker.

As I tear across to opposite corners, I realize how ridiculous I must seem. What's happening here? What's wrong? No music! That's it. There is no music. This is like a Hollywood war epic, but it's just not the same without the music. I can hear my heart in my ears, and every breath is a major event. But there ain't shit for music. It's quiet as a motherfucker sometimes, when you run the edge.

Charlie's guns stay silent. Dong Ha is dumping on 'em again. Now I'm cheering wildly and jumping up and down yelling, "Kill the motherfuckers, kill every one of the motherfuckers!"

The ville is honeycombed with trench lines and fighting holes. All are well camouflaged. On our left flank a long trench line runs parallel to our line of attack. Cows just killed by our prep fires lie in the nearby fields, killed by the tankers. Tankers like to kill shit. I wonder if they painted little cows on their turrets?

I notice a calf standing. As I approach the calf from the rear, I notice that he is shaking and in shock. Large chunks of raw flesh hang from his flanks. His eyes are expressionless. "I'm going to take it out," I tell the S-3. I draw my pistol and walk over to the calf.

I step in front of him and hold my arm straight out. I pop him in his head, twice—real quick. He does not go down. I'm the battalion pistol champ in Cuba 1966, and 2 years later I can't put a calf down. Who is this calf to not go down when I hit him point blank? The S-3 is yelling at me to quit fucking around. I look down and put the barrel against the calf's skull, between the eyes. His skull explodes when I pull the trigger. He drops on me. With a forward jerk he falls into my legs. Laid out in front of me and on my boots, he twitches. I stand there until he stops moving. Then I slowly slide my feet out from under him. I rest my rifle on him as I exchange ammo clips in my pistol before reholstering.

My warrior's dream lies achieved at the tips of my boots. From a time before Vietnam, I had wanted it my way—up close. For the first and only time, I have had my wish. We move through to our next objective, leaving behind our kills.

We move toward another deserted ville that sits atop a slight hill. We swarm over it like ants on a kill—tearing, searching, and milling. Charlie has just been here. We can smell him. He left in a real hurry, leaving mortar rounds, lots of ammo, and food—good rice. We fill a large underground bunker with all the supplies he's left. Our powder monkeys rig it with explosives. We'll blow it when we leave. This place would have been hell to fight for. Oh Jesus, is it dug in.

We are supposed to get our drinking water from the well in this ville. My two canteens had gone dry long before. The whole country, it seems, has gone dry. Less than a year ago, there had been so much water. I had been drenched by the cold mountain rain, the taste of my hair in my mouth from the water running over my head. Now, such heat. Such dryness. The rice fields crackle from it.

At the village well a real dirty-ass Marine from Head-quarters company is using a piss pot for a bucket and the wire that we use to string field telephones for rope. Plunk! The helmet hits the bottom of mud and slime. "Damn thing's goin' dry," he says, big grin on his face, teeth missing. He brings up a load and pours it into my canteen. Shit's like syrup, more green slime than water.

"Hey, how about a little more broth with this mother-fucker?" I say.

"Sure thing, my pleasure, Cap'n," He grins his tooth-less smile. With each helmetful he pours lumps of gunk into my canteen.

I put four halazone tablets in each container. (Two halazones could kill any living thing that could fit in a canteen. I wonder what all that stuff does to me?) The canteens are like cans of soup as I shake them vigorously to dissolve the tablets. Then I root around for a Funny Face packet. My wife would always send packets of presweetened drink mix in her weekly care packages. What was that sweetener? The flavor could send your mouth to another universe. Goofy Grape. Rootin' Tootin' Raspberry. Choo Choo Cherry. I tear open a packet and dump the powder in the canteens.

The green slime makes the Jolly Olly Orange bloom in a real special way. Talk about flavors exploding in your mouth.

After the first sip I try not to breathe. I just try to keep my throat open and let the shit slide down. Kind of like a reluctant blow job. Big slimy chunks like hair out of a drainpipe slide down my throat. I am so thirsty that I drink a whole canteenful.

I can feel that stuff moving around in my stomach. My acids are trying their best, but my stomach is churning from the shit fighting back. Oh no, the halazone's just made that stuff high and ready for a fight.

An hour later the well has refilled itself. Dirty water but no chunks. I wash the slime out of my canteens and refill them. This time I choose grape flavor.

Just before dark the colonel calls the staff together. It is a field ceremony out on a combat mission.

"Captain Spencer, you are completing your service in the Marine Corps. You have been an outstanding officer in this battalion. Your record has and will reflect your outstanding service," the colonel says.

Holy Christ. This is a summa cum laude, my Ph.D. No fancy robes, no marching bands, but this is my education. Just my brothers and I at night in Leatherneck Square. What an arena—right in Charlie's backyard. Kiss my ass, Charlie. Judged worthy by my peers in battle. This is more than I'd ever dreamed of attaining. It is my degree in macho. But it comes too late to have the meaning I had hoped it would have. Macho is a game I no longer want to play.

"Thank you, Colonel," I say quietly. "I am very touched."

We are men standing alone—apart from the rest of the world—honoring one another. We are undertakers at our own convention.

Shut it the fuck down, Ernest. Shut it the fuck down. I look over at Mike and grin. I need to keep my edge.

The battalion is slow to get underway the next day. Everyone is sullen, pissed off, quiet, and inside. We can taste Charlie. Just after starting our sweep, a fight breaks out several clicks away toward the coast. It's the doggies. Boy, do they use arty! They must be trusting suckers, or they are really getting burned. A two-man chopper flies over us, circles, and lands. Clean and dressed in new green utilities, a doggie colonel gets out. He meets with our colonel. They argue for several minutes. The doggie gets in his helicopter and flies back to the fight going on in the distant tree line.

"Fucker just wanted our tanks," the colonel says to me. "I told him: 'You want the tanks, you take this whole battalion of Marines, too.' " The little thick-necked old man is grinning.

Yahoo! Marines to the rescue. We would have run in there smiling. We'd have grinned at the doggies as we saved them. But that doggie colonel is too proud. His pride is such that he will let his men die, and we will live a while longer.

We set off inland. We move up a wide, shallow gully, which is lined with dry, scratchy brush. We move up the gully, away from the dying doggies.

Delta Company is point company and moves up the center of the gully. Alpha Company is on the left and Charlie Company is on the right. Bravo Company is in reserve. The battalion command group is just behind Alpha on the left flank.

I wait at the base of a low ridgeline while the companies maneuver into position. At the base of the hill lies a small stagnant pool surrounded by a thicket of tall brush. I sit there at the pool's edge and play in the water with my hands. In the water I see reflections of clear blue sky and my own image. Under the water my fingers are straight, but they appear to bend toward me. Refraction. I notice pin-thin worms nearing my hand. Leeches. They are attracted to the heat of my fingers. I play with them. As they near, I move my fingers. Little blind fuckers wiggling back and forth toward me. It is hot in the sun, and there is not a wisp of wind.

After climbing the ridge I walk along and watch Delta Company working the low ground below. The point man is on a narrow dirt path. I know this man. He holds his rifle at port arms across his chest. He is not pointing his rifle forward in the usual way. He is a draftee and a conscientious objector. The chamber in his rifle is empty; they are not going to get him to give up his beliefs, but he accepts being a Marine. He is a brother on the line.

I see the puff come out his back. The point man sits down, then falls over. Bang! From 300 yards away, the sound reaches me after the event takes place. "Contact," I yell.

Below me I see the point man's squad leader, Killer, run forward. His tall frame moves in his distinctive loping stride. After looking down at the point man, Killer turns and waves. A machine-gun crew rushes forward and sets up to the left of the dead Marine. I see VC bullets kick up dirt around the machine gun before I hear the firing. Marines rush forward now from all sides. All shit breaks loose. Nobody asks, and no one says go. Marines just jump in like guys who have been dying of thirst and suddenly come upon water.

The ground that I'm walking has not been cleared by the Marines ahead of us. Mike, the communications officer, is on my right.

"Drop back, Mike, and cover our right side," I call to him.

He nods, drops behind to my right, and shifts his stance. One of my S-2 clerks is on my left.

"You cover straight ahead, I'll cover the middle," I say to him.

"Rog," he says. What a salty fucker that kid is.

We are just three Marines, two captains and a lone lance corporal. We become a fire team with everyone carrying an M-16 rifle. High-priced riflemen, but riflemen we are—first, last, and forever.

We walk the low brush like guys on a rabbit hunt. Down below, Delta is pinned down. Grenade explosions and firing are constant. Those familiar incoming cracks start going over me as a heavy machine gun opens up on our command group. Because of all the radios, we attract special attention. The command group takes cover in a bomb crater. I use a small rocket crater that is to the right of the colonel. Mike lies down in the open 20 feet away from me. I am so overcome by a sense of Charlie all around me. The fighting is at a fever pitch, a roar below us in the gully.

"Delta 6 is hit," Ken yells to me. I wonder about my two radio operators, who are now with Delta's commander.

I curl into a fetal position on my left side. I remove my helmet, place it at my feet, and draw my rifle up next to my face. My right hand is on the grip near my right armpit. I'm taking at least one motherfucker with me, I think to myself. If they come, I'm going to zap at least one. Sweat is trickling down my nose and over my chin. Full in the sky, the hot sun beats on me. Without my helmet my protection is gone, but I'll get cleaner shots without it.

Let the motherfucker come, and I'll light him up. I can feel, taste, and sense Charlie. I wonder about this overwhelming awareness. Am I associating with Delta Company?

Tanks move up and into the fight. One tank's flame thrower is not operational, but the tank still runs and its machine guns work. I see a Marine jump on top of the tank to try to guide it. A gook runs out into the open and shoots him right off the tank. The tank commander pops up out of the hatch and starts firing his grease gun; another hidden gook does him. The tanks are in too close to use their cannons.

Charlie Company, on the right of Delta, envelopes into Delta's position. Alpha Company on the left stops and sets up a blocking force, cutting off Charlie's escape route. Charlie is almost completely surrounded. We don't give him a chance to run. We want to kill him. Every fucking one of him. We reach the plateau just above the heavy fighting.

Ken and the command group position themselves to my right to observe the fighting below. Mike has disappeared. I am down on one knee waiting to find out what's next; there isn't sweet shit for an intelligence officer to do at a time like this. An AK-47 on semiautomatic goes off right next to my ear. The first round is behind me and comes from my right. I see the sandy soil explode in front

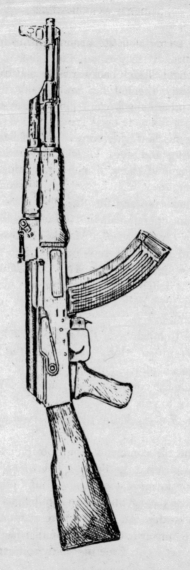

AK-47

of me. The second and third rounds hit in front of me in the sandy dirt.

Instinctively I kick backward like a backstroke swimmer starting. One armed, I'm pointing my rifle toward the firing as I hit on my back, on my pack. An arty radio operator is staring wide-eyed at me, only 30 feet away. I'm aiming at him and he's looking at me. He looks like he's dead and just waiting for it to catch up with him. The gook must have jumped up right behind him and tried to spray us. No one is hit. The fucker missed everyone.

"I see where he went. I'll get him," the arty forward observer says. This arty lieutenant draws his pistol and starts crawling over the edge of the plateau toward where he thinks the gook went. "I'm going to get an R&R out of this," he says while laughing loudly. The poor veteran has gone off the deep end.

"Lieutenant! Goddamn it, Lieutenant, get your ass back here now!" Ken is screaming. He is standing straight up and screaming at the top—beyond the top—of his voice. The lieutenant slinks back. Ken jumps right into his face. Nose to nose, eyeball to eyeball, Ken screams, "Your fucking job is artillery support, goddamn it. You're not a grunt, you understand?" Ken's feet are almost off the ground.

"Yes sir!" the lieutenant says, standing at attention.

As we start to set in nearby, the arty lieutenant comes over to me for consolation. We have known each other for almost a year. Old nice guy Spence lets him down easy.

"Pistols are for jerking yourself off," I say. "Maybe if you'd have taken a rifle, Ken would have thought you were really serious."

The lieutenant looks like a kid that just got cut from the team.

Battalion sets up in a bomb crater again. Bomb craters are everywhere in Vietnam, like parking meters downtown. Someone tells me that Delta 6 has flunked. Dead. I walk over to the colonel, who is talking on the radio to regiment.

"I'll take over Delta Company again, Colonel," I say. My voice is soft, quiet, and matter of fact.

"No, no, Spence," Ken interjects. Ken is looking at the colonel now. "Spence is outta here, Colonel. You've done your time, Spence. Enough."

"Thanks, Ernie," the colonel says. "Ken is right, you've had enough."

I do not protest but walk quietly back to my gear and dig in. A nice deep hole. The sounds of gunfire dying down as nightfall sets in. The sky is dusty and hazy from all the gunfire, grenade explosions, and tanks churning the ground. The pall of death hangs heavy in the still, hot air. Men wait, scattered in random fashion. The forward edge of our perimeter is 50 yards in front of me.

I take all my bearings as darkness comes. I plot who is where and what my fields of fire will be. I get into my foxhole and wait as darkness falls. I wait. Charlie doesn't hit. It is dark, very dark. Overcast. No moon. No sky.

I have a problem. I can feel the screamers coming on. None of this wait business. I have flat got to shit. Now! I crawl out from my hole. I take an entrenching tool and a wad of toilet paper. It has a wrapper on it like new money. There's a sandy spot about 20 feet in front of me. I dig a cat hole with the entrenching tool. Squatting low, I pull my trousers down onto my boots, I lean back so I won't hit my pants. Dogs are lucky—four legs are easier to shit off of than two. Just after I start going real good, an M-16 opens up full blast. One clip on automatic. Green tracers start coming right over me. Like a player in a picnic game, I crawl back to my foxhole on all fours, trousers around my ankles, butt sticking up in the air. The fire fight lasts only a few moments, then silence. No Marines yelling, nothing. A good sign.

After another half an hour, I crawl out and lie down beside my foxhole, my pack for a pillow. I try to remember if I ever wiped my ass. I lie there with the sweat and grime hardening on me like the frosting on a cake. There is occasional gunfire from Delta Company throughout the night. I sleep with most of my switches on.

It does not feel right the next morning. I am beginning to scare myself—my feelings and intuitions are so strong now, so open. Like raw wounds before my mind's eye. I've become a psychic with myself. I know beforehand if something's coming. I've had this sense for some time, but I would not let myself believe. I couldn't. I would have lost control of myself.

It is a Marine tradition to cover up your foxhole before leaving to deny the enemy free use of your work. That morning I just sit at the edge of my foxhole. The others cover up their holes after eating. I do not eat; I sit there waiting. I know it is coming. No longer wondering why, I just sit, smoking cigarettes. All my life I had analyzed, asked why. Now I just sit. Why doesn't mean a thing.

My clerk asks to go down to Delta and if I want to accompany him.

"No," I say. "But find out who got it, OK?"

"Rog," he says chewing his gum in a smacking way.

If that little shit had gotten me a little earlier, I would have pulled his helmet down over his shoulders for him. But I don't give a fuck about discipline anymore—not that kind. There is not a thing wrong with that kid, he is fine. I am the one who is fucked up.

About fifty of our guys have been killed or wounded. Most of them were from Delta Company. Most of the dead had served with me. The first sergeant of Delta stops to talk. He is all jacked up—it's his first time in a fire fight. He brags to me about all the shots he fired from his pistol.

"What'd you hit?" I ask.

"Fuck, I don't know. I wasn't looking," he laughs.

Yeah right, I think. I bet you jerk off with your eyes closed, too.

"Try a rifle with your eyes open sometime. It's just like pussy," I say.

My clerk comes back with a gook machine gun.

"This is the one that did your replacement and a lot of the other guys," he says. "Boy, you should have seen the place! There were dead gooks all over. Tanks ran over some. Plowed the cocksuckers. Boy, did the guys kick some ass down there. This gook had about thirty grenade holes around his little bunker. It was like a little coffin." His eyes light up as he retells the battle.

The squad leader, Oyster, killed the gook machine gunner. Oyster put an M-79 grenade launcher right in his face. Both of my radio operators are OK. "They said to tell you it was close, real close," my clerk says as he walks away.

While everyone is saddling up getting ready to move, the arty lieutenant comes over to talk to me again. "I'm going to completely blow away a whole fucking grid square!" he says. His eyes are on fire, and he has a big mad grin on his acne-scarred face. "I'm going to fucking blow away our objective. When we get there, there won't be anything left!" His eyes look to me for acknowledgment and acceptance.

"Get the fuck away from me, asshole," I snarl, "or I'll wrap my rifle around your head."

We are bracketed by four of our artillery fire bases. They are firing on our next objective, a tree line near the Cua Viet River. The colonel and the S-3 move ahead to watch the prep fires. Then . . . Bang!

I land in my hole. Bang! A guy's on top of me. Dirt is blowing in my open mouth and nose. I had opened my mouth to balance the concussion of the explosions. I taste dirt and smell sulfur from the arty rounds. My eardrums are numb. Oh fuck, I'm dead. I knew it, goddamn it, I fucking knew it. Close to us a guy is screaming his screams of oncoming death. He's being taken out slow.

I hear Crazy Doc yelling, "Somebody check those guys."

"I'll check them," one of my clerks yells from nearby.

"Jesus, Jesus, Jesus," I am saying.

"You OK, Captain?" the guy on top of me asks. He's wrapped around me like a mink stole. His dick is in my right ear, and he's looking into my face.

"Yeah," I say. He jumps out of the hole and is gone. I never see him again.

As I stand up, I notice my clerk standing between the S-4 and a radio operator. They are 10 feet away. The S-4 is laid out on his back, gurgling sounds are coming out of him. The radio operator is curled up and on his left side, facing away from me. He looks like he is sleeping.

"These two are dead," my clerk says.

"That's a negative on your last." The words are spoken by the radio operator, just like he's talking on the radio. Then he goes "Huhhh," real softly and settles into his death.

That sets my clerk to shaking violently. He runs back and jumps into the small crater.

"When are we getting out of here?" My words. Before I realize what is happening, I've said it and said it that way. Three octaves too high and panicked.

"Hold on man, hold on," an arty radio operator yells over to me.

His eyes and mine meet. Shit, holy fucking shit. It's me. I sink back down in my hole. My chin almost on my knees. A wall of shame and a sudden sweat hit. The final truth. I got nailed. I broke.

Arty guys are talking. Rounds have been our own arty, they're saying. One gun fired three rounds out of grid before it stopped.

"Here," yells the arty lieutenant, "I've got proof." He walks over to me with a large fragment from a 105mm arty round—one of ours. "I'll get the bastards for this. I'll get them," he's ranting.

Poor fucker is worse off than I am, and he still has several more months to do. I put on my gear.

I'm in a half daze. I'm floating as I pass the colonel and Ken. They're sitting on a low mound beside the trail.

"Onslow's dead," I say. He was the S-4.

"Shit!" the old man says, stamping his foot.

"Our own did us, Colonel," I say. "Our own artillery did us. Arty just doesn't work with this battalion. Arty really fucking sucks it."

I stumble past them. I want to be up front again. Fuck this staff and command-post duty. When I reach the forward company, I lie down in a narrow trench. A small rain-made trench, 8 inches deep and a couple of feet wide.

Smoke from the arty barrages still drifts upward from the tree line. My head begins to clear.

There are several ARVN soldiers on this operation. They are supposed to know the area, but they are totally useless and lazy. They are dragging ass in the hot sun. We are underway less than 2 hours, and they are completely exhausted. A Marine working with them kicks one of the ARVNs in his ass. Hard. He knocks that skinny fucker about 5 yards. It gets tense, ARVNs glaring at Marines. Everyone is holding their M-16s by the grips, fingers on the triggers, barrels pointing down.

"Easy, easy," I say. "Everybody hold it."

I walk up to them holding my M-16 the same way. I flip my switch onto full automatic. One of the ARVNs has thrown down his flak jacket.

"Pick that up," I say in Vietnamese. "Put it on."

He's glaring. More Marines walk up and start surrounding the ARVNs. He smirks, bends down, and picks up the jacket.

"You don't keep up with us, you don't eat. Understand?" They walk off without saying anything.

"Who the fuck are we doing this for?" a Marine says.

We move into and through our objective without contact. It is early in the afternoon. No Charlie. Charlie is leaving a lot of gear behind, though. Even weapons. When Charlie leaves his weapons out in the open, you know that he's hurting. Trench lines and bunkers are all over the place. If he'd stayed, he could have chopped us down while we were in the open. Jesus, holy Jesus! I set up for the night with Delta Company.

I meet my two radio operators from Delta in a clearing at the center of Delta's position. Without prompting,

Glenn, the talker, recounts the previous day's battle for me. George stands there, white in deep shock.

He tells me how Delta 6 had been cut down by the machine gun. Hit in the legs. Then he was hit in an arm when he raised it. Rodriguez got it through the chest after he lifted Delta 6 on his shoulders. Delta 6 took it through the gourd.

"We were right there, Skipper," Glenn says, his eyes sad and despairing. It was as though they needed some reassurance that it had not been their fault.

"It was just their time, guys," I say softly.

I turn and leave them. Never shaking hands or saying goodbye. They have more time on the line. I am leaving.

I find two trees close together and still standing. The trees are 20 feet from the nearest trench line, the forward position of Delta Company. It is with Delta that I choose to spend my final days. I rig the hammock that I took from the NVA's pack. I always wanted to sleep in a hammock. Charlie can come and kiss my ass if he wants to, but I am going to sleep in Charlie's hammock and out in the open at least one time. I eat double rations of Cs that night before climbing in. I think about the guy whose bed I now sleep in. Fuck you, Charlie. I'm still here.

It is so much cooler up in a hammock. Curled up beneath a moonlit sky, clear and without clouds. I let my legs hang down over the sides. My hands are behind my head. I gaze out over open, deep, black ground until dots of starlight draw my eyes skyward again. Beauty out and far, far away. I am dreaming, and I taste the flavors of life. Restful night and calm dreams.

At first light I get the word that the colonel wants to see me. When I get there he, Ken, and the S-3 are doing breakfast. C-ration ham and eggs, white bread canned, and coffee. The colonel likes to eat. He brews me a cup of coffee on a heat-tab stove.

"The ARVNs deserted last night. We'll be getting a resupply this morning," the colonel says. "This operation is almost over, Ernie. Take the resupply chopper back in. We'll see you in a couple of days."

Ken gives me a wink as the colonel says it. Ken had put him up to it. We all shake hands, and I leave.

On the way back to get my gear, I see Killer. "I'm leaving," I say. "How was the fight yesterday?"

"It was a real good fight, Skip. They hurt us, and we hurt them. A real good fight. A real good fight." His hollow, vacant eyes and washed-out face are testimony to the world he now lives in.

"Good luck to you," I tell him. I'm sure he won't make it. As I walk from him, I realize that he will never make it in Nam or back in the world.

On the way over to the LZ, I stop to say goodbye to Crazy Doc. He gives me the clinical perspective of how the S-4 and Delta 6 died. True to our tradition, I sit and listen to the recounting of the dead. A going-away present for my chest of memories.

A UH-34D helicopter comes in and unloads C rations and ammo, Marine standard resupply. A sniper opens up on us as we're waiting, but he isn't even close. I jump up and onto the helicopter. I stand at the big cargo door on the right side. The engine roars and whines—that bird always shakes before it lifts off. The crew chief grabs my shoulder to pull me back away from the doorway. He lets go when he sees my face—I can get a wild-ass look sometimes. The chopper lifts up and away; the Marines below grow smaller as though viewed through a zoom lens pulling away. Fuck you, Charlie. Fuck you, Marine Corps.

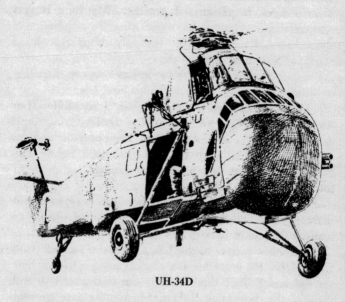

UH-34D

Fuck you, world! The thoughts ring inside me. I'm not going down for anybody. I'm going out on my feet. I've done the full 15 rounds. I took everything that was thrown at me. I could care less about the outcome. I made it! It is not just a short-timer's fantasy.

The crew chief has a disbelieving look. My madman smile must have scared the shit out of him. As we circle into Dong Ha, I sit on a jumpseat against the rear bulkhead. The crew chief is afraid to look over at me. Poor guy probably thinks that I'll turn into a bat and fly away.

After a short briefing at regimental headquarters, I

hitch a jeep back to our rear base at Quang Tri City. My transition back to the world must begin. I have less than a week to get myself together. My time is very short.

Doing Rodriguez

The next day I get word to return to Dong Ha. They are having trouble identifying all the bodies from Delta Company. The Corps likes to have two people who knew the dead do a visual identification. I am one and wonder who else is getting this shit detail.

I meet Doc My Friend at graves registration. He had been transferred to Dong Ha when we pulled out of Khe Sanh. His skin is now a pale bluish white. The dark stubble of his black beard masks his clean, washed face. The bloodshot eyes lie deep and low in the sockets. Holy Jesus, Doc looks awful!

Graves registration is a big green tent next to the runway and just down from the medical center. Poor kid on duty is not fully packed in the head. A real weirdo, almost like the assistant in a monster movie. Everything he says is preceded or punctuated by a semigiggle semisnort.

"Who you guys here to do? He he."

"Rodriguez," Doc says.

The guy refers to a clipboard on a post. "He he, that will be locker 4. Come this way, please."

We follow him past the body-washing table and the hoses. At the back of the tent, a big refrigerator, which is powered by a diesel generator. Roaring fans. The kid opens the door. The body bags are on shelves—feet to my left, heads to my right. He unzips one bag, and I see that the body is wrapped in white, almost clear plastic. The guy pulls the plastic back.

The body's eyes are frozen open. Cloudy gray and lifeless. His mouth is open. His last breath outward, frozen. The tongue hangs out like that of a dead deer. It startles me! I jerk like I've been hit.

Doc is calm. He casually reaches out and pulls Rodriguez's lip up. He confirms the missing teeth.

"It's Rodriguez," Doc says.

"You agree? He he."

"Yeah, it's him."

We sign the death forms and leave. We walk back toward the med center.

"You know, Spence, when Rodriguez first came to the battalion, I did the physical on him. That's how I knew about his missing teeth. He was the type of guy you don't forget. He scared the hell out of me. Rodriguez said he wanted into Delta Company because he said the rap on you was that you had your shit together."

"Well, I guess he was right, huh Doc?" I say in a soft whisper. " 'Cause I just did him." My mouth hangs there, open.

I do not stay and visit with Doc My Friend. I leave without ever saying goodbye. I just want to get out. A tidal wave had just washed over me and consumed me. I am drowning.

To me, Rodriguez represented the Marine Corps. I don't mean the John Wayne Marines. I mean real Marines. Line guys. All the companies have real heroes— guys like Rodriguez. But Rodriguez is gone, and I am still here. Why? Am I but a witness? I feel fear wash through me. They die while I watch. For what purpose? Whom should I tell? Who will care? How long will they care?

I have a dreadful fear that I'm going home all fucked up. I try to get my act together. I don't have much time. Bell rings, and you've got to stop punching. Whistle blows, and you stop hitting. War is not played by such fixed rules. I'd adjusted to different rules so many times that I am no longer sure what I'm doing. All I am certain of is that I do not want any more of war. This is my one clear certainty.

The remaining days are a collage of quiet times spent watching the sun go across the sky. We transfer as a battalion to an area just outside of Da Nang. I pose for a picture with Mike and Ken. All three of us, shirtless in the hot sun, our dog tags hanging around our necks. Arms linked over each other's shoulders. A buddies photo. I think it was Mike's camera. The rest is a blur. I don't even remember the flight out to Okinawa.

Join the Allies on the Road to Victory
BANTAM WAR BOOKS

BANTAM
SHOP-AT-HOME
C·A·T·A·L·O·G

Special Offer
Buy a Bantam Book
for only 50¢.

Now you can have Bantam's catalog filled with hundreds of titles plus take advantage of our unique and exciting bonus book offer. A special offer which gives you the opportunity to purchase a Bantam book for only 50¢. Here's how!

By ordering any five books at the regular price per order, you can also choose any other single book listed (up to a $5.95 value) for just 50¢. Some restrictions do apply, but for further details why not send for Bantam's catalog of titles today!

Just send us your name and address and we will send you a catalog!

BANTAM IS PROUD TO PRESENT A MAJOR PUBLISHING EVENT

THE ILLUSTRATED HISTORY OF THE VIETNAM WAR

Never before has the Vietnam War been so vividly presented. Never before has a full account of the controversial war been available in inexpensive paperback editions.

Each Volume in the series is an original work by an outstanding and recognized military author. Each volume is lavishly illustrated with up to 32 pages of full color photographs, maps, and black and white photos drawn from military archives and features see-through, cutaway, four-color paintings of major weapons.

Don't miss these other exciting volumes: